Multimedia
Cookbook

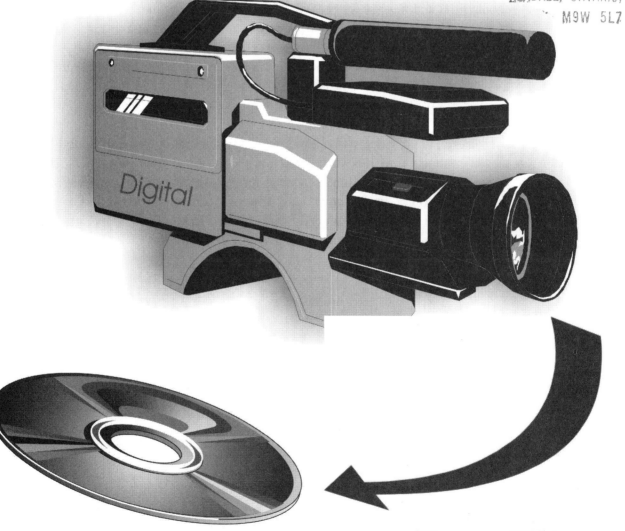

Digital

Dan Titus

How to start and run a video production service

Acknowledgements

Thanks to Steve Yankee for his valuable input about business and marketing. Thanks to Jim Calkins who supported us with information about finance.

Publisher's Note

Printed in The United States of America
Published by Venture Marketing, Chino Hills, California, USA

Titus, Dan
The Multimedia Cookbook: Business Start-up Guide
Includes references and index.
ISBN 1-58291-110-X

Design and illustration by Paul Daniels. Edited by Marilyn Weishaar.

*This book is dedicated to all the
small business owners
throughout the world.*

Foreword

Consumers and professionals now have the tools to create desktop videos and multimedia products — and start their own business!

The advent of powerful computers and high-resolution digital video cameras have exposed millions of would-be producers to videography, which is the art of producing videos. People now have the tools they need to produce economical professional videos and multimedia right in their own homes. Many people trained on their home computer editing systems now aspire to become professionals in the industry. They have trained themselves in video basics. Many have gone on to take classes to enhance their understanding of camera technique and video editing. Hence, they have the basic video skills to work for a company or to start a company of their own. However, if the goal is to start a company, other skill sets are necessary. Enter *The Multimedia Cookbook: Business Start-up Guide.*

The Definition of Multimedia
Webster's Dictionary

Main Entry: *mul·ti·me·dia*
Function: adjective
Date: 1962
Using, involving, or encompassing several media.
Literally, "more than one medium".
Therefore, anything mixing text and graphics is multimedia.
However, multimedia implies: sound, motion and/or animation, video, and/or interactivity.

Example: "a multimedia approach to learning".
- multimedia noun

About the Author

Dan Titus was raised in Southern California. He is a musician, videographer and writer. Dan graduated in 1987 from California State University Long Beach with a Bachelor of Science in Marketing. He has been involved in multimedia business consulting for the past several years and is president of Venture Marketing, a business media publishing firm. When not researching and consulting, Dan enjoys writing songs producing videos, and spending time with his family.

Table of Contents

About The Author

Introduction

Chapter 1: Preplanning

Contents

Chapter 3: Financial Planning

Chapter 4: Marketing

Contents

Chapter 5: The Business Plan

Chapter 6: Copyrights

Chapter 7: Tips & Tricks

Contents

Introduction

Technology in recent years has brought about significant improvements in manufacturing techniques. Coupled with new smaller electronics and faster computer chips, prices for equipment have dropped dramatically. The clear-cut winner are consumers and videographers. More people have access to video equipment. Therefore, more people are developing the necessary skills to potentially start a videographer service. Hence, people may have the desire to start a business but have no idea how to begin.

This book is designed to help you start a videographer service. It is designed to acquaint you with concepts that you will need to form a new business. I have concentrated on the start-up aspects rather than the operational day-to-day aspects of running a service. For example, one of the key topics is how to develop your business plan. I have tried to include elements to address starting a videography service from scratch.

This book has a Web site that accompanies it and is a key element for your success. It is assumed that you have basic camera, desktop video, computer skills, and that you can navigate your way around an IBM compatible system. This is important to get the most out of the Web site, and programs that go with this book.

How to Use This Book

This book is designed to be used as an action plan for starting your business. It is laid out in specific sections to attain this goal. Some of the chapters are grouped; others are specific to one particular topic. Therefore, you can skip around in this book rather than read it in a sequential manor.

Chapter 1: Preplanning

Chapter 1, *Preplanning,* is designed to expose you to a lot of information so that you will begin thinking about all the aspects that lie ahead. It asks many tough self-evaluation questions so that you will have a better understanding of your strengths and weaknesses. The chapter walks you through what will need to be accomplished in order to test the feasibility of your business idea. Explained are the different types of business entities, such as corporations and partnerships. The chapter basically acts as a large preplanning checklist that you can use to get started.

Chapters 2 - 5: Business Plan Elements

Chapters 2 through 5 are grouped together. These are the chapters that explain what is needed to develop a detailed business plan and understand the financial information that will be required in the business plan.

Chapter 2, *The Business Plan Primer*, will introduce you to business plan basics. I will go go over the basic elements needed to create a business plan and explain the primary points that need to be covered in each section of the plan.

Chapter 3, *Financial Planning,* introduces key elements of finance and what you will need to know in order to add some of these elements to your business plan. Jim Calkin is my mentor in this area. Much of the information in this part of the book is excerpted from Jim's book, *Business Buyers Handbook.* The perspective in this chapter is for buying an existing business. However, the elements are the same for any business.

Chapter 4, *Marketing*, shows how to create a marketing plan. A marketing plan is a key element of your business plan, therefore, it is imperative that you have an understanding of the concepts presented in this chapter.

Chapter 5, *The Business Plan*, is a sample plan that you can study to see how all the elements fit together. It is laid out following the outline presented in Chapter 2.

Chapter 6: Copyrights

As a videographer, you need to know about copyrights and how to control the rights of the videos that you produce. This chapter will educate you about basic copyrights and how to protect your work.

Chapter 7: Tips & Tricks

In Chapter 7, *Tips & Tricks,* we look at marketing and operating tips offered by Steve Yankee of *Video Success Secrets*. Steve brings to the table his in-depth knowledge about customer service, corporate identity, marketing, video demos, advertising, and much more. Also included are sample forms and contracts that you can adapt for your business.

Chapter 8: Financing Your Business

Chapter 8, *Financing Your Business*, offers you a quick overview of some of the sources of where you can find money to start your business. From partners, family, friends, government loan programs, to credit cards, this chapter offers strategies to help you get the start-up capital you will need.

Chapter 9: The Web Site

Here you will find an overview of the Web site that is designed to go along with this book. Look for the Web Connect logo, shown above, in the margins throughout this book. This will notify you about expanded chapter topics, books, or software that you can receive online. Simply fill out and return the registration form, which you will find in the back of this book, to qualify for this Web site access.

Appendix

In the appendix you will find reference material, such as bibliography and contact information.

Final Notes

Throughout this book I offer tips that are noted in the margins. Be sure to put your personal notes there too, as this will assist you with your critical thinking.

Again, in order to take full advantage of the software and spreadsheet templates that are at the Web site, and on the CD-ROM, it is assumed that you are able to use a computer, and the associated software for Internet access.

Finally, I hope that you find this book informative and I hope it helps you with your business endeavors.

Dan Titus

Preplanning

This chapter is designed to get you thinking about the many aspects of your new business and what you will need to accomplish from a tactical point. It is designed to test the feasibility of your business idea. From evaluating yourself as an individual to providing detailed checklists, it will help you with preplanning. There are many questions asked and you will need to know the answers before you move forward with your endeavors. Use this chapter as a tool to honestly assess yourself.

The U.S. Small Business Administration (SBA) has compiled a going-into-business checklist, which is designed to help you stay on track. The checklist asks questions that can help reveal fail points in your thinking. Fail points are areas that can have negative consequences once you launch your company. If you can answer these questions thoroughly and positively, you will be prepared to begin the quest of starting your own business. If you stumble on these questions, you may have some more studying to do.

Successful businesses begin with a practical plan. Entrepreneurs need a solid background in the businesses they choose to launch.

The SBA correctly identifies these qualities for a successful start-up:

- A practical business plan — Although not a quality, it is critical to your success.
- The dedication and willingness to sacrifice to reach your goal.
- Technical skills (If you launch a trucking company, you better know about trucking.)
- Knowledge of management, finance, bookkeeping, and market analysis.

Clarify your reasons for launching, and even more importantly identify your strengths and weaknesses. Once you've answered these questions, you'll have a good idea whether you should launch right away, or hold off for awhile.

Why Do You Want to Start a Business?

As a first step, ask yourself why you want to start a business. Identifying your reasons is important. People start a business for different reasons, including:

• Freedom from the daily work routine.
• Being your own boss.
• Doing what you want and when you want to do it.
• Improving your standard of living.
• Freedom from a boring job.
• Having a product or service you believe will create a demand.

Some reasons are better than others. No reason is wrong; but be aware that there are tradeoffs. You can escape the daily routine of employment only to find that business ownership is more demanding.

The checklist asks the difficult questions that can reveal holes in your thinking, that may have dire consequences once you launch your company.

Self-Evaluation

Do You Have What it Takes?

Going into business requires particular personal characteristics. This portion of the checklist explores your personal attributes. It is important to stay objective, and above all, be honest about your capabilities.

The goal here is to access your strengths and weakness, so you can develop a strategy to deal with those aspects of your new business that you will be directly involved with, and those that you will delegate to other parties. You may be great at finance and you may have the computer aptitude to develop your own business promotion kit. However, you may not have the knowledge, or desire, to pursue all the marketing aspects of writing a business plan. Therefore, seek help in marketing.

Personal Characteristics

- Are you a leader? Do others turn to you for help in making decisions?
- Do you make decisions easily?
- Do you enjoy competition?
- Do you have the required self-discipline?
- Do you usually plan ahead? Impulse is a dangerous trait in business owners.
- Do you like to meet new people?
- Do you get along well with a wide range of people?
- Can you delay gratification?

Personal Conditions

This group of questions is vitally important for new business owners.

- Do you have the physical, emotional, and financial strength to launch a new company?
- Do you realize that running your own business may require working 12-16 hours a day, six days a week, even Sundays and holidays?
- Do you have the physical stamina to handle the workload and schedule?
- Do you have the emotional strength to withstand the strain of the disappointments and rejection that invariably come with launching a new enterprise?

Consequences of Launching a Business

- Are you prepared to possibly lower your standard of living until your business is firmly established? It can take time to regain your standard of living if you quit a high-paying job.
- Is your family prepared to go along with the strains they also must bear? Launching without the support of family can kill a business.
- Are you prepared to lose your savings? There's a reason they call it risk. Many people lose their entire investment.

You can escape the daily routine of employment only to find that business ownership is much more demanding.

Be ready to eat, drink, and sleep your new business. Like a newly planted plant, there will be a critical time while your business takes root.
Your time will be needed to develop systems that will help run the busi-

ness. At the same time, you more than likely will be running the day-to-day operations.

Your Business Knowledge

It is unlikely that you possess all of the particular skills and experience that are critical for business success. You'll need to learn as much as you can before starting your business.

• Have you ever worked in a managerial or supervisory capacity?
• Have you ever worked in a business similar to the one you want to start?
• Have you had any business classes in school?
• If you discover you don't have the basic skills needed for your business, will you be willing to delay your plans until you've acquired the necessary skills?

Feasibility

Your business ideas and your market feasibility will become basic elements of your business plan. See chapters 2 and 5 for details about business plans. For now you can make a preliminary outline based on the following criteria. Briefly answer the questions the best that you can. The objective here is to test the feasibility of your business idea.

Your Business Idea

Many entrepreneurs dive into business blinded by their dream before evaluating the potential of the business. Before you invest time, effort, and money, the following exercise will help you differentiate good ideas from those ideas destined to fail.

• Identify and briefly describe the business you plan to start.
• Identify the products or services you plan to sell.
• Does your product or service satisfy an unfilled need among potential customers you can reach?
• Can you make a profit? How long will it take to make a profit?
• Will your product or service be competitive based on quality, selection, price, or location?
• What will it cost to produce, advertise, sell & deliver?

The Market

To succeed, you need to know who your customers are. To learn about your market, you need to analyze it. You don't have to be an expert market analyst to learn about your marketplace, nor does the analysis have to be costly. Analyzing your market is a way to gather facts about potential customers and a way to determine the demand for your products or services. The more information you have, the greater your chances of capturing a profitable segment of the market.

Sometimes the best market information is simply the knowledge you have gathered by being an enthusiast for the market: If you launch a taco stand, a lifelong interest in tacos helps. You can approach this several ways, however, it is critical to learn your market before investing time and money in an enterprise.

These questions will help you gather the information necessary to analyze your market and determine if your products or services will sell.

- Who are your customers and how often will they purchase?
- Do you understand their needs and desires?
- Do you know where they live and how to reach them?
- Will you offer the kind of services that are missing from the market but are likely to be valued?
- Will your service prices be competitive in quality and value?
- Do you know how to promote your service to your target customers?
- Do you understand how your business concept compares with competitors'?

Many entrepreneurs go into business blinded by dreams, unable to thoroughly evaluate its potential.

Business Start-Up Planning

So far this checklist has helped you identify questions and problems you will face determining if your idea is feasible and converting your idea into reality. Through self-analysis you have learned your personal qualifications and deficiencies, and through market analysis you have learned if there is a demand for your service.

TIP
See chapter 4, ***Marketing,*** *to see how a marketing plan is laid out.*

The following questions are grouped according to function. They are designed to help you organize yourself.

Name and Legal Structure

- Have you chosen a name for your business? If so, will you want to trademark the name?
- Have you chosen to operate as a sole proprietorship, partnership, or corporation?

> **Choose a business.**
> **Choose a business name.**
> **Is the business legal?**

Choosing a Business Structure

Once you decide to establish a business, a primary consideration is the type of business entity to form. Tax and liability issues, director and ownership concerns, as well as state and federal obligations pertaining to the type of entity should be considered when making your determination. Personal needs and the needs of your particular type of business should also be considered. The main types of business entities are:

- Sole proprietorship.
- Corporation.
- Limited liability company.
- Limited partnership.
- General partnership.
- Limited liability partnership.

Sole Proprietorship

A Sole Proprietorship is set up to allow an individual to own and operate a business by him/herself. A Sole Proprietor has total control, receives all profits from and is responsible for taxes and liabilities of the business. If a Sole Proprietorship is formed with a name other than the individual's name (example: Center Stage Video), a fictitious business name statement must be filed with the county clerk or county recorder where the principal place of business is located. No formation documents are required to be filed with the secretary of state. The secretary of state is the government agency that controls business entities. Other state filings may be required depending on the type of business and your regional location.

Corporation

A Corporation is defined as a legal entity which separates the liability of the business from that of the owner(s). In other words, the owner(s) of a Corporation cannot be held personally liable for lawsuits filed against the business, and the owner(s) credit cannot be affected by the business debts.

Why Incorporate?

Protection is the chief reason for incorporating. Many people believe that their businesses are too small or too new to incorporate. Others believe that to incorporate would be too expensive. Nothing can be farther from the truth. Here are some benefits of incorporating:

• Provides lawsuit and asset protection.
• Provides tax advantages not available to individuals who obtain businesses or partnerships.
• Avoids personal liability.
• Establishes lines of credit, which are not available to individuals and partnerships.
• Provides easy way to capitalize your business.
• Offers capital for operating expenses.

Limited Liability Company

A Limited Liability Company generally offers liability protection similar to that of a corporation but is taxed differently. Limited Liability Companies may be managed by one or more members. In addition to filing the applicable documents with the secretary of state, an operating agreement among the members as to the affairs of the Limited Liability Company and the conduct of its business affairs is required.

TIP
Nevada and Wyoming corporations have become popular over the past several years because they offer privacy and lower operating costs than offered by many states.

Limited Partnership

A Limited Partnership may provide limited liability for some partners. There must be at least one general partner that acts as the controlling partner while the liability of limited partners is normally limited to the amount of control or participation they have engaged in. General partners of a limited partnership have unlimited personal liability for the partnership's debts and obligation.

General Partnership

A General Partnership must have two or more persons engaged in a business for profit. Except as otherwise provided by law, all partners are liable jointly for all obligations of the partnership unless agreed by the claimant. Profits are taxed as personal income for the partners. Filing at the state level is optional.

Limited Liability Partnership

A Limited Liability Partnership is a partnership that engages in the practice of public accountancy, the practice of law, or the practice of architecture, or services related to accountancy or law. A Limited Liability Partnership is required to maintain certain levels of insurance as required by law.

Your Business and the Law

A person in business is not expected to be a lawyer, but each business owner should have a basic knowledge of laws affecting the business. Here are some of the legal matters you need to be acquainted with. Also, you will find checklists, which are broken out by sections.

* Do you know which licenses and permits you may need?
* Do you know the business laws you will have to obey?
* Do you have a lawyer who can advise you and help you with legal papers?
* Are you aware of Occupational Safety and Health Administration (OSHA) requirements if you have employees?

Do you know about:

• Regulations covering hazardous material?
• Local ordinances covering signs, snow removal, etc.?
• Federal tax code provisions pertaining to small business?
• Federal regulations on withholding taxes and Social Security?
• State workers' compensation laws?

When starting a new business, there are many important decisions to make and many rules and procedures that must be addressed. While there is no single source for all filing requirements, the following checklists have been developed to assist you in starting your business.

Checklists

Federal Government

• Register or reserve federal trademark/service mark.
• Apply for patent if you will be marketing an invention.
• Register copyrights.
• Contact the Internal Revenue Service for information on filing your federal tax schedules.
• Apply for employee identification number with the Employment Department if you have employees.
• Check compliance with federal wage laws.

State Government

• File partnership, corporate or limited liability company papers with the secretary of state's office.
• File state tax forms with the franchise tax board.
• Find out about workers' compensation if you will have employees.
• Apply for sales tax number with the board of equalization if needed.
• Check state wage law if you have employees.
• Observe OSHA safety compliance if you have employees.
• Draft fire egress plan.
• Develop injury and illness prevention program if you have employees.
• Check compliance with health laws if you have employees.

Download the Ebooks:

How to Get a Tradmark

How to Get a Patent

Local Government

• Get any required business licenses or permits.
• Order required notices (advertisements you have to place) of your intent to do business in the community. File DBA, (Doing Business As).
• Get local building permit from building department.
• Fire permits - You must pass fire safety inspection if you have a commercial office. Have fire extinguishes? Fire sprinkler system in place? Note: Periodic fire safety inspections will be required after opening.
• Check zoning laws.

Protecting Your Business

It is becoming increasingly important that attention be given to security and insurance protection for your business. There are several areas that should be covered. Have you examined the following categories of risk protection?

• Fire.
• Theft.
• Robbery.
• Burglary.
• Vandalism.
• Accident liability.

Discuss the types of coverage you will need and make a careful comparison of the rates and coverage with several insurance agents before making a final decision.

Business Records

• Are you prepared to maintain complete records of sales, income and expenses, and accounts payable and receivables?
• Have you determined how to handle payroll records, tax reports, and payments?
• Do you know what financial reports should be prepared and how to prepare them?

Other Tasks

• Open a bank account for the business.
• Have business cards and stationery printed.
• Purchase equipment or supplies.
• Order inventory, signage, and fixtures.
• Get an email address.
• Find a Web hosting company.
• Get your Web site set up.
• Have sales literature prepared.
• Call everyone you know and let them know you are in business.
• Advertise in newspapers or other media if yours is the type of business that will benefit from paid advertising.
• Call for information about Yellow Pages advertising.
• Have business phone or extra residential phone lines installed.
• See if the business name is available for use as a domain name.
• Register the domain name even if you aren't ready to use it.
• Install alarm system.
• If you plan to accept credit cards and bank debit cards, you will need to set up a credit card processing system.

Keep Going... ... Never Quit!

Preplanning

Chapter Notes

Business Plan Primer

Avoid a crash: Plan!

This chapter presents an overview of the basic elements of a general business plan. The outline explained here serves as a template for the sample business plan in chapter 5. Study this chapter and then turn to chapter 5 to see how the basic elements of the plan are developed. This chapter also includes information about how to develop your marketing plan, which is part of the business plan.

If you are unfamiliar with financial reports, you might want to jump to chapter 3, *Financial Planning*, in order to become familiar with the financial elements presented in this chapter.

Business Plan Structure

1. Summary.
2. Body.
3. Conclusion.

Executive Summary

This should be an overview and lead-in to the rest of the business plan. It is a summary of the main topics within the plan. It should emphasize your competence in three key areas: Marketing, technical capabilities, and financial management.

The Business Concept

Describe your product or service. Where possible, supplement with diagrams, illustrations or pictures in the final package you show to prospective lenders or investors. This information can be referenced in an appendix.

Marketing Approach

Provide a brief description of your market strategy and the market segment you will be trying to reach. Outline the channel(s) you will use to reach this market, such as direct mail, retail, or wholesale distributors.

Financial Features

Provide estimated dollar amount of sales and net profits that you project for each of the first 3 to 5 years of operation, then set forth the amount of starting capital you will need. Where cash flow is negative (as is usual) in the first few years, it may be helpful to show your net cash exposure or cumulative negative cash flow for each month or quarter, to show that your initial starting capital will be more than sufficient to cover such maximum exposure.

Start-up Costs

Provide a brief overview of the start-up costs. This is basically a start-up cost schedule and is usually posted to the cash flow section of your pro forma forecasts that are part of your business plan.

Current Business Position

Provide pertinent information about the company, and whether or not it is a start-up venture: How long it has been in operation. The form of the business: proprietorship, partnership, or corporation.

Achievements to Date

Give an overview detailing any major achievements since the company started, or has accomplished to date. Provide examples of patents and prototypes. Also, mention where your facility is located. If you are a start-up venture, mention any of the relevant points mentioned above and/or where you currently are in your planning.

Statement of Objectives

Sell your proposal to prospective investors, discussing the unique advantages your product or service has over existing products and services. State both your short-term and long-term business objectives for the business, and describe the image you want to create for your product or firm.

Qualifications of Principals

Provide your background qualifications to run this particular business, citing education, overall business experience and particularly any successful experience in a closely related type of business operation. Also describe, if applicable, the qualifications of your partners or other co-owners who will be part of the management (or board of directors, in the case of a corporation) of your proposed business.

Background of Proposed Business

Spell out the background conditions of the business in question, including how, where, and when the product is being used, as well as where trends in the business or industry seem to be leading. Also, discuss the main players (i.e., your competitors), or likely competitors, if the venture is a start-up operation. Explain where your business will fit in this picture. Will you be on the cutting edge of what is happening, or just one of the pack that is not in the same league as the market leaders? If it is the latter, you will need a very convincing rationale to show why you can garner enough business to meet your financial objectives.

Product or Service Use

Provide a complete detailed technical description of the product or service to be offered, including a summary of any test data. Describe any tests that are currently planned. Show that you are anticipating the future by outlining any further refinements or logical next steps for developing an improved or different product later (or comparable plans for further innovations in a service business). This is your chance to show that what you have is a better mousetrap and is also technically feasible.

Industry Overview and Trends

Provide an overview of your industry. Detail any discussions that provide simple graphical representations of the current situation in your industry. Mention any trends that are evident in your industry and/or regarding your products. Through research you can analyze your DJ service and your market potential, helping you make informed decisions.

Information for this part of the business plan is available from two sources:

• Primary research - Collecting the data and compiling it yourself.
• Secondary research - Obtaining the information from already published sources.

Strength and Weakness Analysis

This is where you will do your competitive analysis. Prepare a weighting-scoring model in order to evaluate your key competitors. Primary competitors are in the same business that you are, such as, other DJ services. Secondary competitors would be all other entertainers, such as bands, in your immediate target area. The goal is to rank your business in relation to your competition.

When you know how you rank in relation to your competition, you then can form plans and contingency plans to deal with them.

Basically, the model allows an objective overview of subjective information. It allows you to weight specific criteria and rank the importance of criteria. Score the criteria, then, total the scores.

To see an example of a weighting-scoring model, see the strength and weakness analysis in chapter 5, *The Business Plan..*

Marketing Strategy and Plan

Discuss here your marketing plan or strategy. This will include identifying the market segment you are seeking to reach, and the various means through which you intend to reach it, such as door-to-door sales, retail sales, direct mail, media advertising, selling through sales reps, jobbers, or multi-level distributorships, or whatever else you plan to do. If you can, mention the degree of market penetration and market share you expect to achieve, year by year, for the period for which the business plan is making projections (say 3 to 5 years). Create a budget for all the associated costs and include this in the business plan.

The Four Ps of Marketing

Product

Give a detailed overview of your product(s) and/or services. Include any factors that make it different and why these factors are an advantage to your competitors' product. That will differentiate you in the market place. Define all your products or services.

Place

Describe how you will distribute your product or service in the market. Will you reach your target audience by door-to-door sales, retail sales, direct mail, media advertising, selling through sales reps, jobbers, or multi-level distributorships? Describe your primary target location. For example, your service may be located in a under-served region of the county.

Pricing

Describe how you will price your product or service.

Will you use penetration pricing to gain market share or will you price your product as a prestige product, charging a higher price? Are you the only one on the block with this type or product/service? Explain how you arrived at your pricing.

TIP
See page 4.5 for more about market strategies.

For example, when you are operating your service, you might use penetration pricing to drive out a smaller competitor. This "low-ball" pricing strategy can work fine as long as you can still cover your overhead costs. This type of pricing is usually used to increase market share, and is short-term only.

Prestige pricing is used when you want to charge a high price for a high-quality product.

Markup pricing is the most popular method used by wholesalers and retailers in establishing a sales price. When the merchandise is received, the retailer adds a certain percentage to the figure to arrive at the retail price. An item that costs $1.80 and is sold for $2.20 carries a markup of $0.40, or 18% of the retail price. The initial markup is also referred to as the "Mark-on".

Pricing to the competition can be done if it covers your operation costs and still makes a profit. Formula pricing is similar to markup pricing. A fixed value is multiplied by the cost. For example, a restaurant might charge five times the cost for a meal product: 5 x $0.85 = $4.25 selling price.

Psychological pricing is a method to persuade a customer to buy. For example a price of $2.99 for a "value" meal may appeal to a customer who is looking for a discount meal. By charging $2.99 rather than $3.00, the customer perceives value in the product because of the "odd numbered" price. Discount stores and fast-food restaurants use this pricing in conjunction with their primary pricing scheme.

Promotion

How will you promote your product? Discuss in this segment how you plan to go about creating awareness of the product among its ultimate consumers, through advertising, publicity or otherwise, even though most of your sales may be made to middlemen such as wholesalers or retailers.

Cover all methods you will employ, such as telemarketing, circulars, print or electronic media advertising, direct mail, catalogs, or other means. Here it will be useful to include promotion kits, photocopies of dummy ads, brochures or other promotional materials that you may have already prepared, if you feel they will be effective in selling your business plan.

Market Segmentation

Market segmentation is the process of dividing a market into specific differentiated segments that have the same identifiable characteristics so that products and/or services can be designed in order to meet the needs of consumers in each segment. When Henry Ford began producing the Model T, he stated: "They can have it in any color they want as long as it black." His basic marketing strategy was undifferentiated with no segmentation.

Today, car manufacturers recognize a myriad of segments, that taken as a whole, constitute the market for cars. There are segments for hot rodders, mothers with children, young families, status seekers, and even states, whereby government air-quality regulations form a segment.

Forms of Market Segmentation

There are five basic market segmentation forms:

1. Demographic - by age, sex, income.
2. Geographic - by region, urban, or rural.
3. Psychographic - by lifestyle or personality.
4. Benefits - consumer perception: tastes good, feels good.
5. Volume - heavy user, light user.

Organizational Plan

It is important to spell out in a convincing way your plans for structuring the organization, including a description of the key positions and the people who you have lined up to fill them, with their (hopefully impressive) qualifications. Include an operational plan, describing in detail the type, and, if known, location of office and equipment that must be obtained. Also discuss what professional services you will require. For the 3 or 4 key people in the company (including each top person in the sales, finance and technical departments), include their resumes at this point, or place them in an appendix at the end of the business plan, but refer to them here.

Financial and Technical Data

Here is where you include detailed pro forma financial statements and other important data in support of the conclusions you have set forth in other parts of this business plan. (See chapter 3. *Financial Planning*, for a detailed discussion of these topics). These should include most or all of the following:

Profit and Loss Projection

Profit-and-loss projections should be on a monthly basis for the first 3 years, and quarterly for subsequent years, in most cases.

This projection shows your business financial activity over a period of time (monthly, annually). It is a moving picture showing what has happened in your business and is an excellent tool for assessing your business.

Pro Forma Balance Sheets

These should show your projected ending financial picture for each of the periods covered by the P & L Statement, (Profit and Loss Statement).

The balance sheet shows the condition of the business as of a fixed date. It is a picture of your firm's financial condition at a particular moment in time, and will show you whether your financial position is strong or weak. It is usually done at the close of an accounting period. It contains the following topics:

• Assets.
• Liabilities.
• Net worth.

Download the financial spreadsheet that goes with the sample business plan in chapter 5 from the Web site.

Cash Flow Projection (Budget)

You will need to show monthly or quarterly and cumulative pro forma cash flows, which should tie into the P & L statement and balance sheets for each period covered.

• This document projects what your business plan means in terms of dollars. It shows cash inflow and outflow over a period of time and is used for internal planning.

• It is of prime interest to a lender and shows how you intend to repay your loan.

• Cash flow statements show both how much and when cash must flow in and out of your business.

Break-even Analysis

In chart form or otherwise, show the level of sales you will need each year in order to break even for that period.

The break-even point is the point at which a company's expenses exactly match the sales or service volume.

It can be expressed in:

1. Total dollars or revenue exactly offset by total expenses or,
2. Total units of production (cost of which exactly equals the income derived by their sales).

Acquisition Schedule for Fixed Assets

Show an equipment list and loan-dispersal statement about how and when you plan to acquire your equipment. This can usually be appended to the cash flow budget at start-up.

Other Supporting Data

- Technical drawings of product and/or detailed description of services offered.
- Itemization of capital equipment required and cost.
- Pricing schedule.
- Detailed list of prices for products or services offered, in their different configurations.
- Store layout drawings.
- Floor plans or layout of a proposed manufacturing plant, including a manufacturing flowchart and cost estimates for producing the product, broken down into cost accounting detail.
- Tooling or equipment required for production.
- Description of all tooling that will be required, and the estimated costs.
- Market survey data (primary research).
- Provide any market demographic information that you have developed or obtained.

Summary and Conclusions

This is where you make your final pitch, so make it convincing. Tell what your total capital requirements are and how much of a safety margin will be provided. Describe who will put up what debt and equity capital to get the business off the ground, and when each infusion of capital will be required. This will tell the prospective investors how much of an owner-ship interest they will be getting for X amount of money.

Reiterate the amount of profits you expect the business to make, when you will make it, and how much of your own money and property you are putting into the venture as evidence of your commitment.

Most outside investors are likely to be leery of investing unless it is clear that you have put your own financial neck on the line, so there's no chance of you simply losing interest and walking away.

Appendix

This is where you will include an appendix for supporting data. Include whatever you think will be useful to get your point across. You can have more than one appendix.

This chapter has exposed you to the basic elements of a business plan. The next Chapter, *Financial Planning*, will detail financial elements that you will need to know before you can draft your own business plan.

*Download the Ebook, **The Government Loan Resource Guide**, from the Web site.*

Chapter Notes

_____
_____
_____
_____
_____
_____
_____
_____
_____
_____
_____
_____
_____
_____
_____
_____
_____
_____
_____
_____
_____
_____
_____
_____
_____
_____
_____
_____
_____
_____
_____
_____
_____
_____
_____
_____
_____
_____
_____
_____
_____
_____

Financial Planning

When someone offers you a lifetime warranty, ask:
Whose life, yours or mine?
- Dan Titus

In this chapter we look at financial planning. As a video service business owner, you will need to have a basic understanding of the principles presented here. The material presented is from the standpoint of analyzing financial information in order to purchase *any* existing company. This is information you will also use to reinforce your knowledge while you are drafting your business plan. Thanks to Jim Calkins for the use of much of this material from his book, *Business Buyer's Handbook.*

Understanding the Health of a Company

The single most important consideration in your review of the company is understanding its financial health. This is done through analyzing and understanding the standard financial measuring tools describing the company. Without knowing how to do this properly, you will invariably ask the wrong questions and get the wrong answers. This, in all probability, will lead to a misunderstanding and possible disaster on your part.

Over the years a standard measurement procedure has evolved for describing the financial health of a company through the use of two health measuring thermometers namely the Income Statement, and the Balance Sheet, or Condition Statement. Both describe the company in very rigid terms representing a fixed time frame.

I present the subjects by going back to the very fundamentals of why you should have financial statements. You may think that you already know how to read a financial statement, but you better be like the major league baseball player who has been playing baseball for fifteen years. Every year he goes to spring training and finds out again and again, that "this is a baseball, and this is a bat, and the fundamental object of the game is to have the bat hit the ball." Most importantly, no matter how long he has played baseball, he learns something new every year. So it is here. You need to go back to the basics and find out what financial statements are and what to do with them. You are bound to learn something you don't already know.

The Income Statement

To understand income and its effect on the company, you have to start with the very basic reason for the business to exist in the first place: Nothing happens until somebody sells something, albeit a tangible product, or an intangible idea. The meaning here is that you are going to transfer something you have to somebody else in exchange for something. Throughout this chapter, that "something" transferred will be either a physical product or an idea, and that "something" received will be interpreted as cash or cash equivalents, i.e. credit cards, money orders, etc.

The term that was created and employed by accountants universally to define that "something received" is income. My definition as used throughout this chapter is:

Income is the total amount of cash or cash equivalents after payment of applicable expenses received from the transfer of goods or services to a second party.

Throughout this chapter I use the term money as a shorthand description of cash or cash equivalents. Each term, money or cash or cash equivalents is used where the occasion requires. But, in every case the meaning is identical.

Critical Basic Point

In studying the financial health of a company, the number one issue is determining the amount of money the company can generate from sales. This number, properly derived, defines whether or not the company is a viable entity worthy of your consideration, or one that needs a considerable amount of TLC, including an infusion of new capital to become and remain viable. The structures and analysis provided below will help you understand how to get this information.

Over the years accountants have developed a standard analysis structure that makes it easy to determine the amount of money available to the company to pay income taxes (taxable income), and the amount of money available to the owner for future use (cash flow).

SALES/ REVENUES
less
Cost of goods sold or cost of sales
gives
GROSS PROFIT
less
Selling expenses
less
Administrative expenses
gives
OPERATIONS INCOME
plus
Other income
less
Other expense
gives

: ....

TAXABLE INCOME
less
Income taxes paid
plus
Extraordinary income
less
Extraordinary expense
gives
NET INCOME

1. Sales (Revenues)

These names are used interchangeably by different accountants in the preparation of financial statements depicting the present operations of the company. While there is no universal usage of each, in general, the term sales implies the transfer of a physical item, e.g., product, furniture, food, clothing, tools, etc. for cash, and revenues indicates the transfer of intellectual property such as advice, or knowledge, e.g., legal or other professional advice for cash.

Therefore, manufacturers, retailers, and distributors tend to use the term sales, while service establishments, such as lawyers, accountants, and consultants tend to use the term revenues.

In both cases, the term represents the total amount of cash or cash equivalents received during a defined time from the transfer of goods or services that relate to the primary activity of the entity providing the goods/services, seller, to an entity receiving the goods/services, buyer. (Usage generally excludes interest received, dividends, and incidental gains/losses from the sale of non-primary items.)

2. Cost of Goods Sold (COGS) - Cost of Sales

These are also used interchangeably by accountants to identify those costs associated with the transformation of some form of raw material into a saleable product. These are further identified as direct costs, indirect costs, and inventory. Note: In manufacturing companies, the transformation takes the shape of changing raw material into finished goods via the process of physically making something. In distributorships, the transformation takes the form of handling, storing, and possibly, repackaging in preparation for sale. In some instances with distributorships, the original material may be cut, shaped, and/or rearranged before final packaging for sale. In retail and service companies, the transforming of basic material into a finished product is practically nonexistent. Therefore, the major item in determining the cost of goods sold for these forms of businesses is that of inventory and the costs - both direct and indirect - associated with the handling of the inventory.

a) Direct Costs - Applicable to Manufacturers: All the costs directly related to the physical handling of the materials during the transformation production process, including:

• Raw material purchases, including freight.
• Labor directly connected with the handling of the material through production.
• Outside processors performing specific tasks related to the production process.

b) Indirect Costs - Applicable to Manufacturers: All those costs not directly related to the transformation process, but are identified in the support of the processes. They include:

• Supporting labor (maintenance and repair, truck drivers, etc.).
• Subcontract labor (includes all associated costs).
• Utilities for the shop.
• General supplies and tools for the shop.
• Equipment rental.
• Depreciation - (A non-cash expense allocation). Insurance covering the production process and shop employees.
• Other supporting costs that can be legitimately allocated to production processes.

c) Inventory - Applicable to manufacturers and distributors.

Inventory is defined as a cost summation of all of the physical goods connected with the transformation process, including:

• Raw materials not yet used in the transformation process.
• Materials and goods in the process of being transformed into saleable products. Called Work in Process, or WIP.
• Finished products not yet sold.

With distributors the inventory will consist mainly of finished products not yet sold, and, in some instances, WIP where products are further transformed from the original item into different sizes and packages.

As defined above, for accounting purposes, the cost of goods sold is the total of all costs and expenses directly associated with the transformation of raw materials into the saleable products that were sold during a defined period. To determine this:

Start with the value of the inventory (raw materials, WIP charges attached to the transforming product, and fully transformed finished goods ready for sale) remaining unsold at the end of the last accounting period. This is labeled beginning inventory on the current period income statement. To this, you add all of the costs and expenses rightfully charged to the transformation of raw materials into saleable products during the period, both direct and indirect. Next subtract out the total value of everything that remains unsold at the end of the accounting period, labeled ending inventory on the current period income statement. Note: This is done because what you want is the true cost attached only to those units that were sold during the accounting period. Therefore, you subtract the costs of the ending inventory because you have already paid for them, even though the items were not sold, This figure is now ready to serve as the base for the next accounting period with no additional costs attached, i.e., beginning inventory.

For any given period the cost of goods sold is:

Inventory on hand at the beginning of the period (beginning inventory).
plus
direct and indirect costs identified with the transformation and handling of the saleable products that were sold during the period.
less
cost of unsold materials and saleable products on hand at the end of the period i.e., ending inventory.
gives
cost of goods sold during the period under consideration.

3. Gross Profit

This is a term developed by accountants to determine how much of the sales/revenues money remains after payment of the costs and expenses directly associated with the transformation/production of the saleable product and truly represents what is available to the company for other operations. It is determined by:

SALES/REVENUES
less
COST OF GOODS SOLD
gives
GROSS PROFIT

4. Selling Expenses

Costs and expenses that are directly associated with the physical selling of the finished product are selling expenses. They include:

• Sales salaries and commissions.
• Entertainment and other promotions.
• Travel costs of the salespeople and others.
• Advertising, trade shows, and special events.

5. Administrative Expenses

Expenses associated with the necessary administrative functions of operating the company are administrative expenses. They include all normal and ordinary office expenses, officers' and staff salaries, bonuses, pensions, non-cash expenses, plus payments made to outside professionals, e.g., attorneys, accountants, consultants.

Normally, interest expense is carried in this category, however some accountants prefer to show it as an other expense (defined below).

At this point, it becomes important to explain what is meant by non-cash expenses, and why they are included in a financial statement.

Non-cash expenses are expenses which are allowed by the IRS as legitimate deductions for tax purposes, but for which there is no cash expenditure. These include such items as depreciation, amortization, goodwill, and covenant not to compete. A further explanation of each item is given below:

Depreciation is the recovery over a finite time of the purchase/investment costs of a tangible piece of property, (generally termed a capital item), such as a truck, production tool, desk, etc. that has a limited useful life, and is used on a recurring basis by the company in its normal operations. In as much as the company uses these items on a recurring basis in the normal course of conducting its primary business, and as they have a limited useful life which requires the item to be regularly replaced, the IRS allows the recovery of the acquisition costs over a fixed time period through the mechanism of tax savings. The allowed time for cost recovery is rigidly set by the IRS in published tax bulletins. Generally, the allowed recovery time will vary from 3 to 10 years depending upon the particular item, and how it is used.

Because depreciation does not impact the cash needed to support continued operations, (i.e., no cash has been expended) the amount shown on the financial statement is added back to the income as a non-cash item when developing the amount of cash available to the company for future operations.

Amortization is similar to depreciation in being a recovery of allowed costs. However, in this case the item for which the recovery is made is intangible property such as goodwill, covenants given, and/or recovery of the costs associated with a promise given (promissory note), which are not used directly in the primary operations of the company. Although there is no physical wear and tear on the items, they represent an operational cost for which payment was made, or a value was given. Accordingly, they are allowed full cost recovery.

Since there is no wear and tear, the allowed recovery time will vary from a few (5) years to several (30). Similar to depreciation the allowance time is set by the IRS tax bulletins.

Two of the more important items for which amortization is used are a covenant not to compete, and goodwill, which in all probability, you will use if you purchase your company.

A covenant not to compete is a time-limited promise you will get from the owner of the company you purchase whereby he promises not to engage in a similar type of business representing a direct competition to you for a specific period and within a specific geographic area. The time and area will vary greatly depending upon the type of business and its present location. In general, you will be looking for a 5 to 10 year time limit, and 3 to 10 mile geographic limit.

Goodwill is simply a measure of the intangible value of a company developed over its years in business. Basically it is a measurement of how successful the owner has been at developing good customer relations. A value is given because, in a very real sense, goodwill is payment to the owner for doing the hard work of developing a market and strong customer base.

In accounting terms goodwill generally represents the value of that part of the agreed upon price of the company over the book value of the tangible assets held by the company. (See below for definition of book value.) The assigned value is usually shown in the other category of assets on the balance sheet. (See below for explanation of balance sheet.) Since goodwill does have value, the IRS allows it as a deduction similar to covenant not to compete but over a much longer period of time.

The selling and administrative costs and expenses described above are those normally connected with the day-to-day operation of the company, and when deducted from the gross profit will yield what is called operations income.

GROSS PROFIT
less
SELLING EXPENSE
less
ADMINISTRATIVE EXPENSE
gives
OPERATIONS INCOME

As important as operations income is in defining the health of a company, the term does not give the complete picture of how income totally affects the company. To get the complete understanding of the total amount of income available for tax payment and use in future operations, you must account for those income and expense sources that arise from transactions not normally related to the primary income-earning operations of the company, but are necessary to the overall successful operation of the company. These are other income (expense) and extraordinary income (expense).

Other income (expense) items are distinguished from extraordinary income (expense) by being a part of operating the company, but are not directly associated with the primary income earning activities of the company. They are of a recurring nature. In as much as other income (expense) items are a part of the operations of the company they are

....

added to the operations income before determination of income tax. Examples of other income (expenses) are:

• Interest income.
• Recovery of bad debts.
• Gain or loss from the sale of assets, or gains/losses resulting from investments made on behalf of the company.
• Miscellaneous income/expense.

These also can include:

• Fees paid to Board of Directors.
• Investments made on behalf of the company.
• Special purchases or sales made by the company but which are not part of normal operations.

Extraordinary income (expense) are transactions and events that are both unusual in character and infrequent in occurrence. The transactions and events possess a high degree of abnormality, are unrelated or incidental to the ordinary activities of the company, and are of a type that would not reasonably be expected to recur in the foreseeable future. Because extraordinary items are not an ordinary part of company operations and are non-recurring in nature, all applicable income tax relating to the item must be paid separately and apart from income derived from normal operations. Hence, they are added to the income statement after payment of all applicable income taxes due from normal operations, and are added net of taxes associated with the extraordinary item, if any. That is, after payment of income taxes for the specific item. Thus, you are adding after tax items to after tax items.

Examples are gains resulting from money given to the company from a governmental source for relocation or code upgrade, and losses resulting from major casualties such as fires and earthquakes.

Adding other income (expense) to the operations income will yield the amount of income available to the company for future operations before the deduction for income taxes, termed net income before tax or NIBT. All applicable income taxes due from normal company operations are paid from this income. However, to get the total amount of income available to the company for future operations, after payment of income taxes, the after-tax amount associated with extraordinary income (expense) must be added.

Critical Point

Put a bright Post-it note on this section so you can refer to it quickly. There is no substitute for understanding the financial reporting of a business. The information you gain from Income Statement and Balance Sheet study and analysis lays the foundation upon which all your other investigative data will rest. Financial Reports may seem daunting at first, but don't be put off. Study the reports until you see the story that they are telling. Very soon you will realize the simplicity of their presentation.

For any fixed time period, and from an accounting standpoint, the income available for the company for taxes and future operations is derived by:

Total revenues received during a fixed time period from primary activities
less
Cost of goods sold
gives
GROSS PROFIT
less
Selling expenses and administrative expenses
gives
OPERATIONS INCOME
plus
Other income
less
Other expenses
gives
NET INCOME BEFORE TAX
less
Income taxes
plus
Extraordinary income (after tax)
less
Extraordinary expenses (after tax)
gives
NET INCOME

The term net income, therefore, represents that portion of the total revenues, after taxes, and extraordinary items, that are available to the company for the future ongoing normal conduct of business.

Understanding the concept of income and how it fits into the operations of the company is fundamental to understanding the financial health of the company. Therefore, it is summarized again below:

Critical Point

The word income has been generated by accountants as a tool for the purpose of determining the amount of tax you will have to pay on revenues generated from selling your products or services. The term tells you whether you made or lost money from operations, and how much income tax, if any, you must pay.

As critical as income is to understanding the operations of the company, it does not tell you the number you need most in running your company, namely how much actual cash is available to you from the revenues to successfully operate the company.

Critical Point

Simply put: Cash not income runs companies. Therefore, to determine just how much cash you have after payment of all taxes, you must translate the net income into cash flow.

Fortunately, this process is very simple: Add back those line items that represented a non-cash expense, that is, those line items for which you did not have to write a check, such as: depreciation, amortization, goodwill, and covenants not to compete, etc. that you are allowed (under IRS rules) to deduct as expenses to save taxes.

Accordingly, cash flow is determined by:

NET INCOME
plus
Non-cash expenses:
• Depreciation
• Amortization
• Goodwill
• Covenant not to compete
• Other non-cash items detailed in other income/expense and
  extraordinary income/expense, that can be legitimately added
gives
CASH FLOW

Therefore, in evaluating the financial health of a company from an income standpoint, you determine how much cash flow is generated from the sales revenues during any specified time period. Typical examples of cash flow generations from healthy companies will be given following the examination of the other measurable aspect of financial health, namely the condition of the company.

Before presenting those items labeled as representing the condition of a company, it is important to describe exactly what is meant by condition so that as you study the various line items you will better understand why they are there, where they came from, and how they impact the operation of the company.

The word condition of a company closely parallels what you mean in describing the condition of your own body. To be in good physical condition means that you have certain body parts (heart, lungs, kidneys, etc. - assets) that must be present to permit you to survive as a living person. All of these parts must be functioning within specified ranges, that is, not being harmfully degraded by foreign entities (liabilities.) Absent these parts within the specified ranges means that you are not in good condition but, in fact, are sick to some degree.

So it is with an operating company. To be in good financial condition means that the company has all of those parts required to function effectively, and that they are within a specified range. Absent any part within its designated range means the company is sick to some degree.

Those parts that an operating company needs (assets) are:

- Cash.
- Inventory.
- Tools and equipment used to perform the transformation from raw materials to saleable products.
- Physical place to perform the transformation from raw materials to a saleable finished product.
- Means of moving the saleable product to the customer.
- Means of collecting the money from the sale of the product.

Those foreign entities that degrade the vitality of the operating parts (liabilities) are:

- Loans and notes owed to outside entities and/or shareholders.
- Taxes and fees owed to local, state, and federal governments.
- Set asides (accruals) for future payments of loans, taxes, etc.

If the operating parts (assets) are not overly degraded by the foreign entities (liabilities) and can remain within a specified positive range, then the company is said to be in good financial condition.

If, on the other hand, the foreign entities (liabilities) seriously degrade or overtake the operating parts, then the company is sick, or unhealthy to some degree.

For accounting purposes, the names and definitions of the operating parts and foreign entities, and the rules for measuring the degree of the health (condition) of a company have been rigidly defined and applied. These are described below.

Balance Sheet or Condition Statement

The balance sheet, or as used by some accountants, the statement of condition describes the financial condition of the company at a specific date. It is a time snapshot of the general health of the company related to its ability to stay in business and remain profitable.

The universally accepted term for the health of the company at any given time is net worth or book value.

> **Critical Point**
>
> In simple terms, the balance sheet, or condition statement displays the sum of everything the company owns - assets - less the sum of everything the company owes - liabilities. If this difference is positive, then the company has a good chance to grow and be successful. If the difference is small, or negative, then the company is in trouble, and may not survive either in the short or long term.

An examination of the respective portions defining net worth is given below:

> **Critical Point**
>
> As you read through the upcoming paragraphs and the associated definitions of the numbers generated to help you in your analysis, remember that these were developed by accountants as a means of easily defining the operating health of the company. Over the years, these numbers and their method of presentation have been honed and refined to great detail. Therefore, they represent an accurate snapshot of the company's viability. You should become very familiar with the definitions and usage of each factor as they will carry considerable weight in your understanding of the company. Since they are universally accepted and understood by those who operate businesses, I will use names and attendant definitions throughout this book in describing certain points I wish to emphasize.

Assets

Assets are the tangible and intangible items owned by the company that contribute to its general health. In a human they are the heart, lungs, internal organs, skeleton, and other parts that make up the human body. They are characterized as current assets, fixed assets, and other assets.

Current assets are cash and other acquired resources that are reasonably expected to be consumed or disposed of during a normal operating cycle of the company. They include:

• Cash (On hand in the company, and/or in the bank).
• Receivables.
• Trade sources, less an allowance for bad accounts.
• Non-trade sources.
• Loans receivable from officers and other employees.
• Prepaid payments made on taxes, rent, and loans.
• Inventory.
• Raw materials.
• Work-in-process.
• Finished goods.

Fixed assets are those resources company-owned which are normally not consumed during one operating cycle of the company, are long term in nature, and are active in supporting the operations of the company. Consumption usually takes several years with the costs associated with the resource being recovered for tax purposes through the mechanism of an annual depreciation allowance. (See income statements).

Generally included are:

• Real property (land and buildings) owned by the company.
• Vehicles used in the operation of the company.
• Machinery and equipment used in the operation of the company.
• Tools and dies used in the operation of the company.
• Leasehold improvements on the owned real property that are used in the operation of the company.
• Office furniture and fixtures used in the operation of the company.

Other assets are those resources that normally will not be consumed during the usual operating cycle of the company, and are not active in supporting the operating process. They include:

• Deposits.
• Life insurance, cash value, and goodwill/covenant allocations.
• Investments made on behalf of the company.

The total assets owned by the company are the sum of the three categories:

CURRENT ASSETS
plus
FIXED ASSETS
plus

OTHER ASSETS
gives
TOTAL ASSETS

Liabilities

Liabilities are the obligations owed by the company that detract from the general health of the company created by the assets. In a human they are the bacteria, fungus, and other disease causing things that detract from the general body health. Liabilities are characterized as current liabilities, long-term liabilities, and other liabilities.

Current liabilities are obligations for which payment will require the use of current assets, will probably be paid within one year from the current date, and include:

• Current accounts payables.
• Trade payable - open accounts and invoices billed to the company from vendors that supply the materials and services used by the company in the normal conduct of its primary business.
• Non-trade payables - Invoices billed to the company from vendors not related to the primary activity of the company.
• Loans and notes payable - The amount to be paid within the current operating cycle of the company. Called current portion.
• Commissions payable.
• Taxes payable.
• Accruals of future payments of deferred items, such as taxes.
• Salaries.
• Pension/profit sharing.

Long-term liabilities are obligations for which all or partial payment will be made in more than 12 months from the current date and require the use of current assets and/or the creation of other obligations. They include:

• Loans and notes payable to a bank or institution, less current portion.
• Loans and notes payable to officers and others.

Other liabilities are obligations for which payment will, generally, be made in more than twelve months from the current date and require the use of current assets and/or the creation of other obligations. Other liabilities differ from long-term liabilities because they include special types of obligations not generally connected with loans and notes, but are more associated with deferred payment of tax and other obligations, penalties due, and purchase of assets not directly connected with the operation of the company. The total liabilities owed by the company are the sum of the following three factors:

CURRENT LIABILITIES
plus
LONG-TERM LIABILITIES
plus
OTHER LIABILITIES
gives
TOTAL LIABILITIES

Critical Point
As described earlier, the financial health of the company from the standpoint of the condition is simply the total assets less the total liabilities, or:

TOTAL ASSETS
LESS
TOTAL LIABILITIES
GIVES
BOOK VALUE (NET WORTH) OF THE COMPANY

The financial health of a company from the standpoint of condition is determined by a critical analysis and review of the assets & liabilities of the company. From accumulated practical experience, accountants have developed an easy way to perform this analysis by using financial ratios. These are a series of numbers that use various parts of the assets and liabilities to describe whether or not the company is in good health and can survive and grow, or in bad health, probably will not survive unless there is an infusion of new cash, and, in many cases, a new management team.

Numerous ratios have been developed to adequately describe the operational health of a company. They are used for various analytical purposes. However, there are a few key ratios that will give you the basics of what you need to know immediately about the general health of the company under consideration.

Before proceeding with presenting the actual ratios, an explanation of the ratios, their derivation and interpretation is put forth to enable you to have a complete understanding of exactly what the ratio is saying about the health of the company. The names attached to the ratios were developed by accountants and are universal in usage and interpretation. I will first define a series of important ratios and their universally accepted interpretations, then detail the healthy ranges to be used in your analysis.

There are three major categories of operating ratios defining the financial health of the company. These are:

1. Solvency ratios.
2. Efficiency ratios.
3. Profitability ratios.

Solvency Ratios

Current Ratio

Defined as: the total current assets divided by the total current liabilities.

total current assets / total current liabilities

Interpreted as: an indication of the company's ability to service its current obligations. Generally, the value is greater than 1.0. The higher the value, the less difficulty the company has to pay its obligations and still maintain assets that will permit continued growth. A value less than 1.0 indicates the company is over burdened with obligations the company, probably, cannot pay and is in serious risk of not surviving.

Quick Ratio

Defined as: cash and cash equivalents plus trade receivables divided by total current liabilities.

cash and equivalents + trade receivables / total current liabilities

TIP
*Key Business Ratios can be obtained from Dun & Bradstreet. Their report, **Industry Norms & Key Business Ratios**, is a standard reference for industry. Their ratios are developed and derived from their extensive database. Contact them via their Web site: www.dnb.com*

Interpreted as: also known as the acid test, and defines the company's ability to service its current obligations from its most liquid current assets. In this case, a value less than 1.0 implies a dependency on the unscheduled liquidation of inventory or other assets to cover short-term debt.

Current Liabilities to Net Worth

Defined as: current liabilities divided by net worth (total assets less total liabilities).

current liabilities / net worth

Interpreted as: contrasts the funds that creditors have at risk versus those of the owner. A small number indicates a strong company with minimal risk to the creditor's money, implying a high credit rating and ease of obtaining additional debt. Conversely, a high number indicates a greater risk to creditor's money, a lower credit rating, and difficulty in obtaining additional debt.

Total Liabilities to Net Worth

Defined as: current liabilities + long-term debt + deferred liabilities divided by the net worth.

current liabilities + long-term debt + deferred liabilities / net worth

Interpreted as: contrasts with current liabilities to net worth by adding the effect of the long term debt and interest charges on the ability of the company to satisfy creditors. If this number is substantially higher than current liabilities to net worth by approaching 1.0 or greater, then creditors will question the company's ability to continue to service existing debt, let alone additional debt.

Fixed Assets to Net Worth

Defined as: total fixed assets divided by net worth.

fixed assets / net worth

Interpreted as: an indication of the amount of funds the owner has invested in fixed assets. A high number e.g. greater than 0.75 indicates either, a) the company has low net working capital (assets less liabilities) and, in all probability, utilizes excessive long-term debt to fund the assets, or b) the company is probably not utilizing the assets efficiently and has over-invested itself in fixed assets. In both cases, questions must be raised about the ability of the company to survive in the short term.

Efficiency Ratios

Sales to Trade Receivables

Defined as: net sales over a given period divided by trade receivables at the end of the period.

$$net\ sales\ /\ trade\ receivables$$

Interpreted as: measures the number of times the trade receivables turn over in the period included for determining the net sales, normally one year. The higher the turnover, the shorter the time between sale and cash collection. Allows a direct comparison of the company to industry norms. If the number is higher than industry norms then the company has achieved a relatively strong position in its market. That also indicates the quality of the receivables is better than the norms. If the number is lower than industry norms, then both the trade receivable quality, and the company's market position need to be reviewed to determine continued market viability.

Day's Receivables

Defined as: the sales/receivables ratio divided into 365 days.

$$365\ days\ /\ Sales\ Receivables\ Ratio$$

Interpreted as: the average number of days it takes to collect the trade receivables. A large number (60 days) means the company may have little control over its receivable collections and be forced to use new debt instruments to maintain production.

Sales to Net Working Capital

Defined as: net sales over a given period divided by net working capital at the end of the period.

net sales / net working capital

Interpreted as: indicates how efficiently the net working capital (defined as current assets less current liabilities) is utilized in the production of sales. A low number in comparison to industry norms indicates under-utilization of working capital, while an exceptionally high number makes the company vulnerable to hostile takeovers. (Net sales are the total sales less discounts given.)

Sales to Inventory

Defined as: net sales over a defined period divided by the inventory at the end of the period.

net sales / inventory

Interpreted as: defines how efficiently the inventory is managed. Serves as a guide to how rapidly saleable goods are being moved, and the corresponding effect on cash flow. A low number in comparison to industry norms indicates an unwarranted accumulation of inventory, and a needless expenditure of production funds. An exceptionally high number could signal difficulty in meeting customer demands on a timely schedule by depleting inventory stocks.

Profitability Ratios

There are three profitability ratios that define the company in terms of its financial health and its value as a candidate for your consideration. These are:

Return on Sales

Defined as: net income divided by net sales during the accounting period, which is normally one year.

net income / annual net sales

Interpreted as: the fundamental earnings number and indicates the profits earned per dollar of sales. A number above the industry norms indicates a superior company and one that is extremely healthy. A number below industry norms, while not necessarily indicating a sick company, indicates a need for further examination of the causes of the below averages number.

Return on Assets

Defined as: net income over a given period divided by total assets at the end of the period.

net income / total assets

Interpreted as: the key indicator of the profitability of the company. A high number indicates an efficiently run company, while a small number indicates a poorly run company.

Return on Equity

Defined as: net income over a given period divided by net worth at the end of period.

net income / net worth

Interpreted as: the ability of the company's owners to realize an adequate return on their invested funds. The higher the number, the more valuable the company is to both the present owners and potential buyers.

All of the foregoing in this chapter have been devoted to giving you the essential factors and their definitions as they relate to the health of a company. At the end of this chapter is a table of norms for the indicated industries. I will also give some key personal observations about what constitutes a healthy company, and which you may find useful in your search and analysis.

The industries focused on are:

• Retail.
• Distributors/wholesale.
• Manufacturing.
• Personal service.

Critical Point

A note of extreme caution: within each of the general business categories given below, individual companies will vary significantly. A low income, or ratio, for a given company, may indicate a better business opportunity than one one having a high income and ratio. Always remember, as critical as the financial data are, they are not the only parameters that should influence your final buy, or no-buy decision.

Here are a few of my observations regarding the analysis and purchase of companies obtained from my personal experiences. They are offered in no particular order, simply as additional inputs for your consideration.

1. In general, a strong healthy company will show a gross profit of 40 percent or more. While not necessarily a deal killer, a number significantly less than 40 percent needs to be examined closely before final decisions are made. A small gross profit could be as simple as allocating some expense line items that are normally shown in selling or administrative categories as cost of goods sold, or the company could be over charging of direct labor, material purchases, or leased equipment. In either case, a more detailed examination needs to be made to ensure you know exactly why the numbers are the way they are.

2. Always make sure the seller gives you copies of his financial statements willingly and without a long, detailed explanation of why the various line items show the way they do. Also, he should not hesitate in giving you at least the current and last 3-5 years of statements. Extreme Caution: If the owner says "What do you need statements for? Look at what the company has bought me: a new house, a new car, a boat at Newport, a summer estate in Maine, and put all of my kids through college," then he, with a high degree of probability, is taking unreported money from the company, and/or not showing all legitimate expenses on his statements. In which event you'll be in serious trouble if you take over and try to straighten out the books. In this event: run, don't walk,

because you could easily wind up in trouble with the IRS for something you had no control over.

3. While the statements do not need to be audited and certified by an accountant per se, they should be prepared by a certified public accountant (CPA). This is critical since a good CPA will not risk his license and ability to make a living by knowingly falsifying data for a client.

4. In addition to the internal financial statements, always get copies of the company's income tax returns and compare them with the financial statements. The two documents, in all probability, will show slightly different data because of dissimilar requirements of each. However, the income tax return should include a section on reconciling the two documents. If it doesn't, find out why, and determine how significant the lack of the reconciliation is. If both documents are prepared by the same CPA, the reconciliation will be in the tax return.

5. You should be able to easily determine from the statements exactly how much the seller is taking from the company.

You will find that the vast majority of business owners you talk with are totally honest, and are anxious to put a deal together. They will give you everything you ask for with little difficulty. Nevertheless, you must always be on your guard until you can verify everything.

Break-even Point

The break-even point is the minimum amount of sales a company must make in order to pay all of its operating expenses, before a profit can be made.

To calculate the break-even point, all that has to be known is what your total overhead is and what your direct costs are as a percentage of sales. The formula is:

fixed costs / 1 - variable costs as a
percentage of sales

How to Calculate the Break-even Point

For example, Sam's Restaurant is a sole proprietorship that was expected to gross $200,000 last year.

1. Separate and list fixed and variable costs

Fixed Costs (FC) - Are costs that do not vary with the volume of business. These include items like wages, rent, and utilities.

Variable Costs (VC) - Are costs that vary with the volume of sales of the business. Examples include: Food, condiments, and paper products.

Fixed Costs

Labor	$38,000
Payroll tax	3,800
Insurance	800
Rent	9,000
Accounting	500
Bank service charge	150
Utilities	7,000
Telephone	1,300
Interest	800
Advertising	1,000
Depreciation	1,800
Miscellaneous	1,200
Total Fixed Costs	$65,350

Variable Costs

Food & paper products $77,000

2. Divide total variable costs by total sales:

$$\$77,000 / \$200,000 = 0.39$$

3. Subtract total variable costs as a percentage of sales from one

$$1 - 0.39 = 0.61$$

To determine the annual break-even point, divide the result into the total fixed cost:

$$\$65,350 \ / \ 0.61 = \$107,131$$

5. To find the daily break-even point divide the annual break-even point by the number of days the restaurant is open in a year.

$$\$107,131 \ / \ 256 \ \text{days} = \$418.48$$

6. Determine if the store is operating above the break-even point:

a) Annually

Annual gross income - annual break-even point

Annual gross income	$200,000
Less annual break-even point	107,131
Total	$92,869

b) Daily

Daily gross income = Annual gross income / total days open

$$\$200,000 \ / \ 256 = \$781.25$$

The conclusion is that Sam's Restaurant is operating well above its break-even point.

Chapter Notes

Marketing

Marketing is the cornerstone of any business. It is a key element of your business plan and is key to your ongoing operations. This chapter is designed to introduce you to key marketing concepts and strategies. If you have not already done so, review the section titled, *The Four Ps of Marketing* in Chapter 2, which starts on page 2.5. This chapter expands on that information.

How to Create a Marketing Plan

There is one vital tool that stands between success and failure with your business: The marketing plan. Many businesses blindly grope their way to sales while others strategically locate their buyers. It isn't hard to see which will work better.

The plan of marketing your business is far more powerful than it seems. It leads you in a definite direction backed with specific research. Marketing shouldn't be a guessing game. It should be a strategic equation with solutions that propel your business forward.

Your marketing plan should never end. It is ongoing, not a one- time activity. So exercise your business and it will grow to be strong and healthy.

The main reason business owners don't pull together a marketing plan is simply that they often don't know how. Here is a guide to help you through the process and help you put together a road map to your business goals.

Every marketing plan has these key elements:

1. Defining the business that you are in.

2. Assessing your competition.

3. Marketing strategies.

4. Understanding what your business is and where it fits in.

5. Discovering who your buyers are and then locating them.

6. Reaching your buyers and exercising your plan.

7. Evaluating the results.

Buy a notebook for this specific purpose. Don't get fancy with your marketing plan in the beginning. It's important to let the ideas flow as they will and not be forced to fit into a particular format. Use your notebook to scribble, draw pictures, and take notes until your marketing plan begins to take shape.

After you have the key elements and their structure you can organize them into a nice, tidy format. A marketing plan should be revised subtly every month and drastically every six months, which means that you will always need a notebook on hand. Marketing is a process that once put into action requires tweaking, changing, and downright overhauling to make it perfect. Times change, consumers change, environments change; that means your business must change in order to thrive.

Buy a small tape recorder to talk to in your car and to pop on in the middle of the night when something hits you and it will. Ideas generate ideas. The more you work with your plan, the more your plan will work for you. The problem will begin to be putting all the ideas to use, not coming up with ideas in the first place.

Defining The Business That You Are In

It is important for you to define the business that you are in. The Disney Company failed to clearly define the business that it was in, and as a result in the 1980s its business and stock value suffered. Disney has amusement parks, produces movies and other multimedia products, manages sports arenas, hotels, and much more. However, back in the 1980s there was no clear defining factor that pulled all of these entities together. It was not until CEO Michael Isner announced that, "The Disney Company is in the entertainment business", that the persona of the company changed. Likewise, it is important for you to realize the business that you are in.

a. Are you in a video business?
b. Are you in a service business?

The correct answer is b.

A video business is a service business.

Assessing Your Competition

Often when we go into business we don't like to think about our competition and because they are the "enemy" we don't really want to acknowledge that they exist or could possibly be doing anything right.

The problem with this thinking is that it gives your competition an ever-increasing amount of power.

Smart business owners know who their competition is, what it is doing and if it is lucky, how it is doing it. They know their competitions' motto, its logo, its customer service ideal and how they reach its buyers.

Simply put, they know as much as possible. Don't kid yourself into thinking that you don't have competition.

Trust me, very few new businesses are original. If you are one of those very, very few...lucky you, because that is the ideal situation, although still fraught with its own difficulties. So gather your courage, admit to having competition, and let's see what the competition has to teach you and make you more powerful.

First and foremost, identify who they are. This is often easy online by simply doing a search of keywords in the search engines. Who came up? What are they doing that is the same as your business and what are they doing that is different?

Make a list of every single aspect you can discover about your competition. Who are they? Where are they? How do they process sales? What methods of payment do they have?

How fast does their Web site load? What are their meta tag/keywords? Who are their customers and/or agents?

What are they doing better than you? How can you improve on this aspect? What are you doing that is better than they are? How can you shift your niche market so that it isn't exactly the same? What are their prices? How do those prices compare with your own?

Ask and answer every conceivable question you can possibly think of about your competition and try to improve your own business so that you are the only conceivable solution.

Finally, keep your competition in your peripheral vision.

Don't forget they are there. Continue to monitor their business methods. It's your best offensive move.

Overview of Market Strategies

Are you the market leader in your industry? Challenger? Do you plan to use a nicher strategy and deal with segments of the industry currently being ignored?

You need to understand and provide a detailed account of what strategy you will use and how you will implement it. The following is an overview of basic market strategies.

Market Leaders

The market leader is the main player in any market with the most market share - the biggest piece of the total pie. For example, Coca-Cola Company is the market leader in the soft-drink industry and McDonalds is the leader in the fast-food market. The primary objective of dominant players is to remain number one. This objective may be accomplished through:

1. Expanding the total market size.

- **New users** - Target customers outside of primary market segment.
- **New uses** - Real estate videos.
- **More usage** - Frequent customer purchasing promotions.

2. Protecting current market share.

- **Innovation strategy** - Introduces new product ideas. Is the leader in promotional strategies. Takes the offensive against all competitors.
- **Confrontation Strategy** - Engages in price wars, promotional wars. Succeeds through intimidation.
- **Harassment Strategy** - Hires away key people, bad mouths, applies political pressure, and other illegal or unethical practices, including under-the-table hardball.

3. Expanding its present share of the market.

Profitability tends to increase with market share. It is better to have 90% of the 10%. A difference of 10% in market share may be accomplished by a difference of about 5 points in pre-tax return on investment (ROI).

Businesses with market shares above 40% earn an average ROI of 30%, approximately three times that of firms with shares under 10%.

However it is expensive for the dominant firm to increase market share in a market where it is already the clear leader. Furthermore, other competitors in the market will fight harder if they are facing a diminishing market share.

Market Challengers

Market challengers are firms that occupy the second, third, or fourth place in an industry. They are "runner-up" companies. Examples include: Pepsi Cola Company and Wendy's Restaurants. Runner-up firms must attack the leader or another runner-up firm if they are to increase market share. The market challenger has three basic strategic alternatives:

1. **Direct Attack** - They can go right for the leader, perhaps with direct product discounts or with a promotional campaign.

2. **Back-door or Blindside Strategy** - Basically the challenger "runs" around the dominant firm rather than attacking it directly. For example, the challenger specializes in tight retail markets that the leader will ignore because the region doesn't meet its traffic requirements.

3. **Guppy Strategy** - Attack a smaller competitor and obtain market share at its expense rather than taking on the market leader. If a smaller restaurant goes out of business, then market share can be increased.

Within each of these strategic alternatives the market challenger has a number of tactical alternatives:

- Discounting Price - Equal value but lower price.
- Lower quality - Lower quality of service but much lower price.
- Prestige - Higher quality, higher price.
- Concentration - Greater concentration of venues.
- Intensive Promotion - Similar to price war but with advertising and sales blitzes as the primary focus.

Market-Nichers

Unless you have millions dollars to launch your business, consider a market-niche strategy. Market in such a way that you become irresistible to your buyers. For instance, instead of selling water, sell bottled water in 10 different flavors. The best flavored, most nutritious bottled water in the world. Now you have a niche. When people think of flavored water, they will think of you.

Make notes. Where can you slice the pie so that what you are doing is specialized and therefore separates you from the masses? Every business has a niche possibility. Consider what yours are. Instead of selling gifts, sell candles. Instead of selling books, sell cookbooks. Get the idea? Now play with it and see what you come up with. What can you do to sliver off a niche of your market and then specialize in it?

Almost every industry includes a number of minor firms that operate in some segment of the market to avoid clashing with larger competitors. An example is Shasta Cola and private label colas found at local grocery stores. The ideal market niche would have the following characteristics:

• Profitable size.
• Growth potential.
• Neglected by major players in the market.
• Defendable against major players in the market.

Some examples of how a market-nicher can be successful are:

• Locate in under-served markets - Inner city.
• Specialize on specific segment - Weddings and school events.
• Focus on one market segment - Corporate business events.
• Customized service - Offer DVDs.
• Service features - Better equipment.
• Unique location - Unders-erved, neglected region.
• Usage Segmentation - Based on light users versus heavy users. This is an example of the 80/20 rule of business, whereby 80% of business will come from 20% of the customers. The goal is to find the other 20%. In the case of your band service, find the 20% that are not repeat customers of established businesses. Then, address this population with a promotional campaign.

The market-nicher is a practitioner of the concept of market segmentation, utilizing multiple dimensions in the delineation of markets.

Discovering What Your Business Is and How It Fits In

This is very important. Your business is a small business. That doesn't mean it won't become a big business. It might even grow to become a corporate business. But right now, it's a small business. You wouldn't put adult size clothes on a toddler. Don't do the same to your business. In the same way that adult clothes would not fit a toddler, so corporate-sized solutions won't fit your small business.

Make the most of what you are. You can't mass advertise like your corporate other, but you can reach targeted audiences through articles in the right publications. You can overcome corporate deep pockets by acting like a small business and offer human solutions, more service, friendliness, one on one, and much more. Understand who you are and develop your strengths. It will be your strengths that pull you away from your competitors and differentiate your services.

Discovering Who Your Customers Are and Locating Them

So who are they? Who, specifically are the people who would buy your product or service? Start with what you are selling and answer the obvious. Are you selling baby clothes? Then your buyers are most likely to be women between 20 and 35.

How expensive are the baby clothes? If they aren't expensive then your buying audience may be younger, couples with less money. Blue collar workers. If the baby clothes are quite expensive, then your audience might be dual working couples in an older category. Professional white collar couples. See how this works? Define what you know about your potential customers. Understand who they are personally and their habits. Evaluate what income bracket they might be in. What do they do in their spare time? What magazines do they read? What newspapers? Think like a potential customer.

Help yourself out by subscribing to the trade publication specific to your business. Every single industry has one, even funerals! Find yours by going to the local library or, better yet, university library and seeking out directories of trade journals. This will become an invaluable resource for staying on top of selling trends and what your buyers are doing.

Join online groups that share an interest surrounding the service or product of your business. This is where niche marketing will really help you out because people love to talk to people who love all the same things they do. Follow them. Listen to them. Join them. And learn from them.

Buy books about your trade, buy mainstream magazines around your trade, buy the publications that your competition advertises in, and read, read, read. This is immensely important as it teaches you about your buyers. Keep a healthy section of your notebook about all the things you learn about your buyers and finding them will become easier and easier. You have to know who they are. You have to understand them before you can find them and sell to them.

Reaching Your Buyers and Exercising Your Plan

Now you know who your buyers are and you're learning more about them everyday. The next question is how will you reach them? What methods will you employ to get your service in front of them? Online businesses have several avenues including:

Internet Newsgroups and Mailing Lists

Join the lists that include your buying audience. Participate wisely by supplying valuable information and responding to requests quickly. Always use an email tag and your Internet address as this will serve as your ad.

Email Advertising

Purchase opt-in advertising. Opt-in advertising is where people agree in advance to be involved in the email list by permission. You can customize a sales pitch that goes directly to the email boxes of your targeted buying group.

TIP

You can locate potential customers online by using Internet search engines. One favorite is: www.google.com

Join a musicians' trade association.

Newsletter Advertising

Advertise in newsletters whose subscribers are your buying audience. In other words, the people most likely to be interested in your service or product.

Article Writing and Ezine Submission

Write and submit articles to newspapers and magazines. Don't forget Internet Ezines, which are Internet magazines. All readers may potentially be interested in your products or services.

Write a Newsletter

Write, maintain, and build your own subscriber base by writing a weekly or bi-monthly newsletter.

Create a Web Site With Reciprocal Links

Create a Web site and exchange links with Web sites that compliment, but don't compete, with your business. Network!

Strategic Alliances

Align yourself with people who can push your product or service for you, who will stand behind you by referring business to you.

Yellow Pages and Word of Mouth

Place an ad in the Yellow Pages. Research your competition there. Encourage word-of-mouth referrals by asking your clients who they know that would be interested in your services or products.

Press Releases

Get the word out regularly to the media. Article space in publications out performs ad space ten times over.

Business Cards

Every time you go out make a point of giving out at least 3 business cards. Make sure your Web site address is clearly and boldly printed on it. If possible, use both sides of your business card. Be creative.

Direct-Mail Copy

Put together a direct mail package about your business and mail a predetermined number of copies to targeted groups each month. See promotion tips on the next page.

Inform clubs, associations, organizations, and interested entities about what you do. Offer them special discounts. In the end it will pay you back tenfold.

Now that you have some ideas about how to reach your buyers, put together a plan that you will follow without fail every single week. Persistence builds momentum. Stay with it and the sales will be yours.

Create a Power Point Presentation

Portable computers are a great way to showcase your material. Simply create a Microsoft Power Point presentation, and show this to your prospective customer. This software, which is basically an electronic slide show, is easy to learn.

Evaluate the Results

Finally evaluate the results of your marketing efforts. Consistently ask your clients how and where they heard about you. Keep a detailed record of which marketing methods are bringing in the most business and give more attention to the winners. Marketing takes diligence and observation.

Drop the methods that are not performing and increase methods that are working well. Don't make a decision based on one ad. For instance don't drop newsletter advertising if the first campaign doesn't work. Make a decision based on 10 ads. Then if it doesn't work, look to other newsletters that might bring in better results rather than dropping the newsletter method as a whole.

....

Video Business Promotion Tips

First impressions are everything. You only get one chance to make them, then it's over. Being ready at all times is the key to advanced sales. If a potential customer asks about your service you must be prepared to hand them a business card and if possible a brochure. You can be the best band in the world, but if you are not ready for opportunities, you will starve. A professional image is a must for any business. Therefore, it is important to spend some time putting together your primary offensive sales tools:

1. Business cards.

Business cards are your first line of offensive attack. Always have plenty of them with you at all times. They are cheap and are a great way to promote your business. You can pass them out at most any occasion and the business that they generate is invaluable.

2. Promotion kit.

Your second line of offensive attack is your promotion kit. Promotion kits are traditionally pocket portfolios. The pockets have space for pictures, promotion brochures, and price sheets. Although these make for a nice presentation, I recommend that you budget the money for a full-color brochure. Brochures provide a degree of professionalism, which can help with your overall promotion efforts. They are much cheaper to mail. Therefore, you will save money in the long run.

Good promotion text copy must contain a brief biography of your business and how long you have been in business. A good biography must answer these questions:

Q: Who are you?
A: Your business name.

Q: What kind of service do you provide?
A: Professional video services.

Q: Why are you in business?
A: To help satisfy demand for video services.

TIP

Brochures are expensive to print and can become obsolete if contact information changes. Therefore, put your contact information on your bio and/or price sheet. Reference the reader of your brochure to these documents. For example say, "See our price sheet or Web site for current contact information."

Q: Where are you located?
A: List the city in which your primary office is located and all contact information, including: address, telephone number, and Web site address.

Q: When are your services available?
A: Outline briefly when your service is available. Example: Weekend events and holidays only.

Stress the benefits that your service provides. Examples might include:

• Professionalism: Number of years in business.
• Top event produced: Celebrity events.
• Equipment: Name brand cameras, editing and lighting systems.
• Top references and endorsements: Quotes from satisfied customers.
• Pricing: Economical pricing.

A good promotion kit will have a video tape or DVD that will showcase your material. With the advent of digital video and price drops for computers and editing software, production of these kinds of materials is becoming very economical. A short 10-minute presentation is all that is needed and will provide a potential customer an overview of your serices.

3. Your Web site.

Your Web site is a basic extension of your business and in many cases the first contact with potential customers. Mirror your company persona across your Web site. Use the same graphics at your site that you use in your other promotional materials: Company logo artwork. This will reinforce your band service in the mind of consumers every time they see it.

Always ask if the contacts have Internet access. If they do, invite them to visit your Web site if they have not been there previously. If they have specific questions that can be answered at the site, direct them to it. Be sure to get their contact information before you refer them, so that you can place a follow-up telephone call at a later date.

....

Direct Sales

Qualify Your Potential Customers

Time is money and money is time. Therefore, it is important to budget the time that you spend with customers. You need to qualify each sales call so that you can proceed with closing the sale. You can screen your sales calls with these questions:

TIP
See page 7.9 for details about direct mail programs.

• How did you hear about us?

Use this question to gauge and measure your promotion efforts. Record the respondents answer on a tick sheet that can later be tabulated in a spreadsheet. Your goal with this question is to find out how your promotion efforts are working by measuring the results. For example, if you passed out 200 brochures at an event and you received 25 telephone calls as a result, your cost per lead generated would be the total cost of the flyer, divided by the number of calls:

Measure Your Cost Per Lead

cost per lead = cost of flyers / number of telephone calls

cost per lead =

(200 flyers x .07 copy charge + ad development charge) / 25 calls

$14.00 copy charge + $40.00 = $54.00 total flyer costs

$54.00 / 25 = $2.16 per lead

Use a code number on your promotion media so that you will know where sales leads are generated. For example, you can buy a cheap numerical rotary stamp and stamp your flyers with a specific code number in a box predetermined on the flyer. When customers call and mention that they have a flyer, ask them for the promotion code, and then log it. Thus, you have a control point on your cost-per-lead program. You can use this same method for display ads:

Cost for ad / number of calls

$375 / 50 calls = $7.50 per lead

• What is your budget?

This question is designed to filter the respondents willingness and ability to pay for your services. They may be willing to purchase your service; however, they may not be able to pay for it and vice versa. They may be able to pay for your service, but be unwilling to pay the price that you are asking. If you charge $1,800 for a minimum 4-hour event and the customer can't afford it, send them a brochure so that they will have your contact information for next time. It is not necessary to contact them again, except for mailings from your mail list and direct-mail campaign. Let them contact you.

If a respondent has an established budget that meets your minimum service requirements, you have a solid lead that warrants investigation. If the person begins by asking for a price concession, you must deal with the objection. Remember, you have a solid lead with this kind of respondent. You can deal with price objections by touting your service benefits, which are outlined in your promotion kit or brochure.

Close the Sale

Once you overcome all objections, it is time to close the sale. You must still get the business. Ask, "Are you ready to get started?" If the answer is yes, send them a brochure and contract to return along with the appropriate deposit.

Marketing Feedback and Improvement

When you close the sale, you are not finished with your marketing effort. You need to continuously improve your service. One way to do this is by providing a customer survey questionnaire. Your survey should have questions to rate your performance and at the same time query the customer as a reference. If the survey is a favorable one and the customer agrees to act as a reference for your service, you win a valuable resource. Provide the survey at the end of each job or mail it to the customer. It is best to get the customer to complete the *customer follow-up survey form* immediately at the end of the job. This will increase your chances of getting the information back with no follow-up necessary. Follow-up calls cost money.

TIP
See page 7.20 for example customer follow-up survey form.

Typical Customer Questions

Here are some typical questions that customers have. Use a defensive sales strategy by being ready for customer questions and objections in advance. Write additional questions that they might have, and come up with a FAQ (Frequently Asked Question) sheet that you can give to each customer in advance. Include this sheet as part of your promotion kit.

May I see a sample of your work?

You can send a video tape, DVD, or show a Power Point presentation. They are a great way to introduce your service to potential customers and prequalify them.

What kind of experience do you have?

TIP

See page 7.18 for example event planning sheet form.

Offer to send a brochure or complete promotion kit if you feel it is necessary. Follow-up with a telephone call. Ask, if there any questions that you can answer. Proceed to close and book the sale. This coupled with an *event planning sheet* plan will be your keys to success. Your professionalism here will pay off.

Do you have references?

TIP

Update your references often. People have short memories. Therefore, you want references that are current and still excited about your band service.

References are standard with any promotion kit. If you are asked for references send a brochure with reference information or direct them to a page on your Internet Web site. Keep the URL for this page unlinked so that you can direct them to it verbally because you don't want to bother your references with too much traffic. For example, a URL might look like this:

www.centerstagevideo.com/references.htm

Once they have the information contact them within a few days with a follow-up call to close the sale.

Do you provide a written contract?

It is very important to confirm your booking in writing. Terms should be clearly defined to avoid future problems. It is simple to refer a potential customer to a unlinked page at your Web site that has this information if they insist on seeing it in advance.

TIP
A sample contract is available on page 7.18

Do you have liability insurance?

This is an important question and one that you should be ready for. Refer the potential customer to an unlinked page on your Web site, or send a current copy of your insurance policy for review if requested.

How will you dress for my event?

It is important to query potential customers about their needs. You must dress the part by dressing formal, semi-formal, or casual, according to your customers' preference. However, be sure to inform them that themed events and special costumes will require additional coordination and therefore, most likely additional costs.

Do you have backup equipment and backup personnel?

Even professional audio and lighting equipment can fail on occasion. Don't let this put an early end to your event. Make sure there is backup equipment and be sure there is a backup band should an emergency or illness occur. You can make arrangements with a competitor if you do not have additional personnel resources.

Do you belong to a professional musicians' association?

If you belong to a professional association, tell people. This will add to your professional persona and increase your credibility. There are several associations that offer services that can assist with your endeavors. Check *www.google.com* to find them via the Internet.

Chapter Notes

The Business Plan

It's sad, but many people are not exposed to the concept of a business plan until going for their MBA (Masters in Business Administration) in college. If I had my way, students would not be able to graduate high school without at least a basic understanding of the elements of a business plan.

In this chapter you will find a sample business plan. Be sure to read Chapter 2, *The Business Plan Primer,* and Chapter 3, *Financials*, so that you will have the necessary footing to draft your own plan using the plan represented here as an example.

Studies indicate that one of the primary reasons that a start-up business fails is because no business plan was developed, and more importantly, implemented. A business plan is basically a road map so that you know where you are going. Many people, and many consultants, believe that a business plan is nothing more than an equipment list and basic costing information. While these are certainly important, they are only very small pieces of the whole puzzle.

Business Plan Benefits

Some of the business plan benefits are:

- Provides you with an operating blueprint.
- Assists with the financing of your business. Your banker or investor will insist on seeing your plan.
- Assists with your negotiations with agents, event planners, and campus personnel.
- Provides a powerful business navigation tool. Defines the business goals and objectives. Allows for plan adjustment - Make your mistakes on paper, it is cheaper!
- Provides a powerful negotiation tool.

If you have ever drafted a business plan, you know that it is a major feat. No one can draft a better plan than you. Sure, there are professionals that can do it for you; however, you are the best person to judge for yourself the current status of your own desires, goals, and financial situation.

There are many stand-alone computer programs on the market that promise a business plan in just hours. While these programs are good at providing general insight into business, they will not provide you with the research necessary to complete a detailed business plan. Can you imagine one of these programs doing a good job if your chosen business happens to be chicken farming in New Zealand? Or, if your chosen business is a entertainment band operation?

You can waste a tremendous amount of time trying to take the easy way out. There is really no simple way. You need to participate in your own future by doing a business plan for yourself or providing the necessary information for a professional consultant to do it.

If you do not have the time or resources to do your own plan, be prepared to spend between $2,500 and $3,500 to have the plan prepared for you.

Depending on the amount of research, this fee can go even higher.
The outline used in this plan is simple. Most business plan outlines are
similar. However some are just too detailed and verbose for my liking.
My strategy is KISS i.e., keep it simple stupid (an acronym used by business people).

This sample business plan will provide you with a template to start constructing your own business plan. Take your time and study the table of
contents outline; then, thumb through the plan to familiarize yourself
with some of the topics.

Where do I start?

You begin with the business plan financials because the bulk of the plan
is written directly from the financial schedules. For example, the
Financials Features Section is derived directly from the Pro Forma
Income Statements. Pay attention to the assumptions on this schedule -
and all of the other financial schedules because they document the thinking behind the numbers. Study the cell formulas of the financial spreadsheets to see how the assumptions tie into the overall statement. You can
use the financial statements in this plan as a model or build your own.
Remember that the financial portion is the backbone of your plan. Start
with financials and then write the rest of your plan.

*You can get get
sample financial
spreadsheets at
the Web site.*

This is a Project

You have to look at this as a project. You must break the project down
into manageable steps given your most precious current resource: Time.
As aforementioned, start with the business plan financials. Once you
start, you will find that the sales forecast numbers feed the revenue portion of the Pro Forma Income Statement on the spreadsheet. In other
words, when numbers are input into the sales forecast, they are automatically posted to the Income Statement. Next complete the expenses part of
the Income Statement i.e., cost of goods sold, operating expenses, and
taxes. Then, you will be two thirds of the way done with the financial
section.

In the meantime, begin to construct the body of the business plan. Start
your marketing plan. Study your primary competition - the services in the
same business that you are in. Study your secondary competition. For
example, DJs and other forms of entertainment. Think about your busi-

Project management task scheduling software is available at the Web site. Use this electronic "To-do list" to budget and keep on track!

ness concept. All of these questions can be answered and plugged into the text body of your plan while you are working on other parts of the plan. If you have a number of band members or partners, assign each of them different portions of the plan. Take advantage of the skills of the people in your group; maybe there is an accountant or a marketing specialist. If so, use those skills.

Your business plan is basically an educated guess in many ways. That's the whole idea. You are minimizing risk by creating a plan; that's what pro forma means. It's a forecast, an educated guess. It's in your best interest to put everything on paper so that any mistakes can be made on paper where they are much easier - and cheaper - to correct.

Enter Murphy. Murphy's Law states: "... if anything can go wrong it will." Try to anticipate anything that can go wrong in advance. Identify these fail-points. Don't be afraid to offer one, two, or three back-up plans. For example, you might say "... we have identified a shortfall in revenues in the third quarter in year 2. However, observations have shown that the county fair is in operation for 12 weeks during this same period. We have forecast sales based on the demographics derived from the fair population, and believe that we can post an added gross based on 4 additional gigs that we can obtain."

The important thing is to answer all of your questions and above all, answer all the questions to the best of your ability. That way you will have confidence in your plan when you are finished.

Sample Business Plan

The remaining pages illustrate a sample business plan that you can use as an example to create your own plan. This plan follows the same format presented in Chapter 2, *The Business Plan Primer.*

Download this sample business plan from the Web site. In popular Microsoft Word format, you can use this as a template to create your own business plan. Also available is the Microsoft Excel spreadsheet that was used to create the financials that go with this business plan. You can edit this information, too.

Executive Summary

The validity of this business concept, as exemplified in this plan, illustrates a strong potential for success. The plan communicates leadership ability by its operators as evidenced by their business and educational experience. The plan's strong marketing analysis and financial features further identify the operators' business and technical abilities.

The entertainment business maintains long-term growth. Therefore, we see a trend in this area for several years. Growth potential is the essence of this plan because it secures a revenue base from which to operate and profit returns for the future.

The Business Concept

Center Stage Video will open with the primary goal of providing video services. Market niches will include weddings, live band promos, semnars, sports, interviews, trade shows, instructional , and special events.

Marketing Approach

We will reach our market through mobile services by traveling to appropriate job destinations. Our primary promotion tools will consist of co-op advertising, display advertising, direct-mail advertising, and personal selling.

Financial Features

Pro Forma financial statements have been prepared for the first 3 years of operation and include: Income statement, Balance Sheet, Monthly Cash Flow, Cash Flow, Revenue Estimates, and Depreciation Schedules. Three-year annual profit-and-loss summaries have been prepared, which exemplify revenue growth.

The summary of annual profit and loss is as follows: Year 1 start-up annual profit after taxes is estimated at $50,313 on total revenues of $88,730. Totals for year 2 are revenue of $93,365 and net profit after taxes of $53,126. Year 3 shows revenues of $131,605 net profit after taxes of $79,981. Pro Forma figures are summarized here.

Summary Figures ($)

Year	1	2	3
Revenue	88,730	93,365	131,605
Expenses	18,446	19,180	21,513
NIAT	50,313	53,126	79,981

All forecasts are predicated on data gathered from studies done from observations and personal interviews with event planners, agents, school, and video companies in the area.

Start-up Costs

Total start-up costs are estimated at $32,045. This figure includes $27,945 for equipment, $1,000 for initial promotion and first installment payment of $6,00 for liability insurance, which is $1,200 annually. See page 5.19, *Start-up Cost Schedule*, for details.

Current Business Position

Center Stage Video is a new start-up venture, which will be operated as a sole propritorship. The purpose of the business is to provide event video services. This plan outlines the validity of this venture by providing a review of the current market, and presents our business concept. We have $40,000 of investment capital to start this venture: $25,000 is from from personal savings and $15,000 is from a loan.

Achievements to Date

- Marketing concept has been developed.
- Capital funding has been secured.
- Equipment has been specified and selected.

It must be stressed that the owners of the business will be putting up $4,000 from personal savings, thereby giving them a equity position from the start of this venture.

Statement of Objectives

We plan to improve on the existing and successful operations already in the marketplace. There are many video companies in the area. However, we know through our research that the majority of these companies are not our direct competition because they only cater to an occasional wedding or special event. We have developed short- and long-term objectives

Short-term Objectives

- Produce enough revenue to cover costs of operation.
- Create customer awareness of our service.

Long-term Objectives

- Our goal is launch and then refine our concept for the first year. The first year is planned as a proving ground.
- If our concept, financial estimates and planning are on target, we plan to expand into club dates within the first few months.

Qualification of Principals

Jim Johnson: Jim holds a bachelor of science degree in business marketing from California State University, San Diego, California. He is an accomplished cameraperson and video editor who has worked for several coporate video production companies for the past several years.

Judy Johnson: Judy is a computer graphics artist, and editor. She holds a associates degree in computer graphics and media design. She has experience as a cameraperson and lighting technician.

Background of Proposed Business

More and more clients are relying on video services as the primary form of capturing their events. Weddings, corporate functions, private parties, and school functions all currently use video services. Therefore, the industry is in a steady growth mode. There is increased competition in the industry; however, this competition is fragmented based on:

• Experience.
• Professionalism.
• Business stability.

The players in this arena are primarily competitors who are divided into three camps:

• **Part-time amateur videographers:** Their target market is weddings, private parties and school functions. These are mainly hobby people in the business for fun.
• **Part-time professional videographers:** Their target market is weekend functions: Weddings, business functions, private parties, and school functions.
• **Full-time professional videographers:** Their target market includes full-time venues such as coporate videos. Included in this section are special events, such as weddings, live band videos, private parties, and business functions.

We will concentrate our efforts in the part-time professional videoagrapher category. We plan to work weekend jobs to start, then move into higher level production as we grow the company. We will differentiate ourselves by offering a degree of professionalism not offered by our competitors.

Industry Overview and Trends

There are over 5 million weddings every year in the United States. More than half of them hire wedding videographers. This equates to more than 2 and a half million videos produced per year. The average price for a video is a thousand dollars. Therefore, the wedding video industry is generates over 2.5 billion dollars annually.

Strength and Weakness Analysis

We have used a weighting-scoring model (WSM) to analyze the competition as well as analyze ourselves.

Basically, the model allows for an objective overview of subjective information. It allows you to weight specific criteria and rank its importance; score the criteria, then, total the scores. The score range is 0-5. The final scores are placed on a scale, which is made by multiplying the lowest score and the highest score. Competitors were scored based on observations and assumptions. Our analysis ranks the market players as a weight percentage.

CRITERIA	WEIGHT(%)
Years in business	20
General video experience	25
Marketing experience	20
Camera experience	10
Financial management experience	5
Financial resources	15
Editing experience	5
TOTAL	**100**

The overall goal here was to see how we stack up against the competition. The scores for all players, including our company, have been tabulated.

We have identified three competitors in our area:

1. Video Productions is a part-time armature video service. It has been in business for 3 years. It concentrates on occasional weddings and local videos for live bands. The company does not operate as a legal business entity and is in business, at this time, simply for fun. This business scored a 1.25 on our weighting-scoring model out of a maximum score of 5 points. Therefore, we do not see this band as a major competitor in our market.

2. That Special Moment is a full-time professional wedding video service, which is operated as a sole proprietorship. The company has been in business for 3 years. The company scored a 3.25 on our model. Therefore, we see it as a viable competitor in our market.

3. Video-To-Go! is an event planning agency that has an entertainment division. This corporation books events and draws from its division talent pool. They sub-contract many of the video shoots and then do post production in-house. The company scored a 4.25 on our model. Therefore, we see it as a viable competitor in our market.

4. Center Stage Video scored a 3.30 on the model. Here are the summary results:

Company Strengths and Weaknesses

Our company's strengths and weaknesses can be identified using the weighting-scoring model.

Our strengths are as follows:

* General video experience.
* Marketing experience.
* Financial resources.

WEIGHTING-SCORING MODEL

BUSINESS	SCORE
Video Productions	1.25
That Special Moment	3.25
Video-To-Go!	4.25
Center Stage Video	3.30

High confidence is evidenced in core entertainment experience and marketing experience. It is important to utilize these key skill sets to gain and maintain market share in the region, which in turn will add to the successful number of years in business.

Our weaknesses are as follows:

• Years in business - zero.
• Financial management experience.

Marketing Strategy and Plan

Market Strategy

Center Stage Video will embrace a "nicher strategy" as its marketing strategy. This will allow the company to operate in a market segment, which will avoid clashing with larger competitors. The ideal market niche will display the following characteristics:

• Profitable size.
• Growth potential.
• Neglected by major competitors.
• Can be uniquely served by the market nicher.
• Defensible against major competitors.

In order to meet these characteristics and still maintain a profitable size, the ideal region to address is the San Bernardino County, California, market. This is an inland region and is neglected by many of our competitors. Therefore, the region is under-served and will fit the nicher strategy that we will be embracing. We will be successful in this market because we will be:

• Locating in new and under-served markets.
• Specializing geographically.
• Focusing on a specific market segment.
• In a unique location.

TIP
See the section
***Overview of
Market
Strategies*** *on
page 4.5 for more
details about
marketing strate-
gies.*

Market Segment

Our strategy is to segment our market into two primary categories:

• Geographic: By region.
• Benefits: Customer perception of our service.

As previously mentioned, our target market will be addressed through our niche strategy, which will address the region of San Bernardino County. We will also stress the benefits of our service in advertisements and in our personal selling efforts:

• Price.
• Image and professionalism.
• Quality.

We will address the following event segments, for the most part:

• Weddings.
• Business events.
• School functions.
• Private parties.
• Live band videos.

The Marketing Mix

We will utilize a marketing mix in order to:

• Define the service.
• Reach specific market segments through the appropriate distribution channels.
• Price the service.
• Successfully promote the service.

The Service

We will position our service around our central positioning theme:

The Complete Video Solution.

Product Positioning Model

Four scenarios follow and include the elements of price and quality:

We have determined that high-value positioning is the best way to address the needs of our customers in our target market segments.

Our primary service will be video and editing services. We will augment these services with one-off duplicaton services.

We plan to offer an extensive music selection to our clients. This is evidenced by our commitment to a varied song performance lists. We believe that music program material is the heart and soul of our operation and is one way that we have chosen to differentiate our service in the marketplace.

PRODUCT POSITION	PRICE	QUALITY
Rip-off	High	Low
Discount	Low	Low
Prestige	High	High
High-value	Low	High

The Place

Distribution

We will reach the target market through live video event recording and post production editing. We will operate the day-to-day office functions within a home office.

Download the equipment schedule, which is in a Microsoft Excel spreadsheet, from the Web site.

Location

We will concentrate our efforts on clients located in San Bernardino County for the following reasons:

- Location of the venues in reference to the owners' homes.
- The chosen market region.
- The under-served attributes of the market.

Pricing Strategy

We surveyed competitor prices for the development of our sales forecast. Our pricing goal is to offer a service that addresses each customer's perception of value. For example, for the city of Ontario, which has a large Latin population, we have decided to institute an *odd* pricing scheme for wedding dates because this population is generally price-sensitive. Therefore, we will price our service by reinforcing the perception of value to this demographic segment. We will price a standard wedding package at $895 rather than $900 in order to reinforce price value.

The pricing for our wedding videos was obtained by averaging the amounts charged by our competitors in the area.

Pricing Schedule

Silver Plan Option

Pricing Includes:

- Two video cameras locations at ceremony.
- Ceremony only.
- Includes 2 hours on location.
- Wireless microphones.
- Custom edited long version of ceremony.
- Ceremony highlights version set to your choice of music.
- Interviews with Bride and Groom.
- Three VHS copies in customized hard case.
- One DVD copy in hard case.
    Total Cost $895.00

Gold Plan Option

• Two video cameras locations at ceremony.
• One video camera at reception.
• Includes 5 hours on location.
• Wireless microphones.
• Custom edited long version of days events.
• Wedding day highlights version set to your choice of song.
• Interviews with Bride, Groom and family.
• Three VHS copies in customized hard case.
• One DVD copy in hard case.
    Total Cost $1495.00

Platinum Plan Option

• Two video cameras and operators at ceremony.
• Two video cameras and operators at reception.
• One video camera at rehearsal and dinner.
• Includes 8 hours on location.
• Wireless microphones and lights (if needed).
• Custom edited long version of days events.
• Photo/Music Video Montage includes 75 of your photos.
• Wedding day highlights version set to your choice of song.
• Interviews with Bride, Groom and family.
• Three VHS copies in customized hard case.
• One Hollywood Style DVD with custom chapters and hard case.
    Total Cost $2595.00

Extended Services

• Additional copies of DVD $50.00 each.
• Additional copies of VHS $25.00 each.
• DVD Authored with interactive menus (Hollywood Style) $185.00.
• Photo/Music Video Montage includes 75 of your photos $275.00.
• Overtime after included hours - $100 per camera per hour.
• One copy of unedited footage on VHS $50 each.
• Second video camera with operator (Ceremony) $300.00.
• Rehearsal dinner coverage 2 hours $200.00.

Discounts

We will offer discounts for casual events based on coupon specials. However, our revenue projections do not allow for much concession here because of the commodity nature of the pricing in the business.

Promotion Strategy

Parameters

- The promotion budget will be distinctly limited.

- The marketing philosophy reflected in this plan emphasizes market segmentation and sharply defined target markets, which are available from our customer profile demographics. Scarce marketing promotion resources will only be invested in high-return segments.

- This plan focus is on the introductory phases of initial opening and secures a budget for continued promotion within these segments.

During the start-up phase of the business, the goal will be to build service identity. This will concentrate around the initial service rollout. The objectives will be:

- Build awareness of our service.
- Present and enhance image of our service.
- Point out a need and create a desire for our service.

The promotion will explain what the service is, what our service has to offer, why we are in business, where we are located, when people can obtain our services, and how people can reach the business.

We will be using pull strategy in order to obtain client awareness of our service. Advertising will be the primary vehicle used to accomplish this goal.

Media Planning

To date, local advertisers have been contacted and are assisting with marketing ideas. We have established an initial rollout budget of $1,000 with a monthly ad budget of $200 to spread across different media:

- Local penny saver.
- Local newspaper - schools.
- Flyers/coupons.
- Co-op advertising.
- Promotional events.

Promotional Budget and Creative Planning

Ad design will be targeted at each demographic segment. Most advertisers will create an ad as part of their overall package. A sketch and logo artwork will be supplied for their use in designing and distributing the ad.

The following chart outlines our advertising/promotion budget.

Media Promotional Budget ($)

Media	1 X Cost	Weekly	Monthly
Brochures	700		
Wedding news			75
Direct Mail		15	45
Co-op ads			60
Table tents	300		
Coupons			20
News Publicity			
Total Costs	**1000**	**15**	**200**

We have designed a four-color full-page brochure. The cost of this is $700 for 2,500 pieces. The brochures will be our primary marketing tool. We also ordered 2,500 table tents, which will be distributed on table tops at events.

Co-op ads are exchanges and trade-outs with local merchants. We will distribute their coupons if they distribute ours. We will also cooperate with in-group advertising efforts whereby we will share ad space with other local businesses that complement our services. We have budgeted

$60 per month for co-op advertising.

We have budgeted $75 per month for classified ad space in wedding event planner publictions.

Publicity is basically *free* advertising. We will provide articles about entertainment related topics to the news media for publication in their newsletters and/or newspapers. Because publicity has an estimated value, it will be an important component to our promotional campaign.

Creative planning and production costs are included in the budget. Artwork for the flyers and coupons will be developed. Most advertisers will create an ad as part of their overall package.

Organizational Plan

Owner/Managers

See page 5.7 for details about owners.

Consultant

CBM Systems will consult with us regarding financial issues and assist with our computer bookkeeping system.

Manuals and Procedures

We plan to operate our business by ourselves. However, as we operate the business we plan to write a personnel manual, which will establish policy and general guidelines for all employees, if and when we hire them. Also, we are in the process of writing an operations manual in order to establish basic procedures. This manual will serve as a training tool and serve as a continual reference, which will address government requirements regarding:

- Hazard awareness.
- Fire safety.
- Illness and injury prevention.
- OSHA (Occupational Safety and Health Administration) requirements.

Capital Equipment Budget

We estimate that equipment will cost $6,465. This figure includes sound and lighting equipment, and office equipment.

EQUIPMENT LIST SUMMARY ($)	
Video & Sound equipment	23,030
Lighting equipment	2,370
Office equipment	2,545
TOTAL EQUIPMENT	**$27,945**

Financial Projections

Overview

Projections have been prepared as evidenced by the following schedules. We have prepared a complete set of financials for year 1, year 2 and year 3:

- Sales Forecast.
- Pro Forma Income Statement.
- Pro Forma Balance Sheet.
- Cash Flow Statements.

We have $25,000 from savings to invest in this venture. We have secured a loan of $15,000 from a private investor. This amount is enough to cover our start-up costs, and provide enough for operating capital.

Income statements serve as operating statements. These give an overview of all revenue and expenses. They also serve as a operating budget for this start-up venture. Refer to the schedule on page 5.6, *Summary Figures,* for the following discussion.

We anticipate low revenue for the first month of operation. However, we anticipate revenue to pick up as we secure contracts with booking agents. NIAT figure accrues on the Pro Forma Balance Sheet in the cash line item. If possible, we expect to pay off the capital loan of $15,000 in year 2; however, the financial statements currently reflect a loan payment schedule for this amount through year 3. This interest amount is considered in the expense section of our Profit and Loss Statement and the principle amount is denoted on the Balance Sheet.

We will build a substantial equity position of $83,669 at the end of the first year. This figure jumps to $132,212 by the end of the second and $207,611 in the third year. These figures represent accruals of revenue and are here primarily for illustration. We will likely draw a salary, which will change these figures.

Our figures represent a positive outlook for our operation. We believe that this will put us in a good position to invest accumulated profits and equity into other ventures and investments in the future.

START-UP COST SCHEDULE ($)

Equipment	27,945
Licenses and tax deposits	200
Phone and utility deposit	300
Legal/accounting	200
Business Fees & Setup	1,500
Insurance	600
Advertising	1,000
TOTAL COSTS	**$32,045**

Summary and Conclusions

The video business is poised for sustained growth. We see a solid growth trend in this area for many years. This growth potential is the essence of this plan because it secures a revenue base from which to operate and secures profit returns for the future.

The owners will commit $25,000 and an additional $15,000 in loans to the fruition of this venture. The strong equity position of this endeavor secures a solid base for operations and provides a sound financial foundation for the future.

The validity of this business concept as exemplified in this plan illustrates a strong potential for success. The plan communicates leadership ability by its operators as evidenced by their business and educational experience. The plan's strong marketing analysis and financial features further identify the operators' business and technical abilities.

Chapter Notes

Copyrights

As a videographer, you need to know about copyrights and how to control the rights of the videos and content that you produce. This chapter will educate you about basic copyrights and how to protect your work.

What is a Copyright?

A copyright is a form of protection provided by the laws of the United States (Title 17, U.S. Code) to the authors of "original works of authorship," including literary, dramatic, musical, artistic, and certain other intellectual works. This protection is available to both published and unpublished works. Section 106 of the 1976 Copyright Act generally gives the owner of a copyright the exclusive right to do [and to authorize others] to do the following:

- Reproduce the work in copies or phonorecords.
- Prepare derivative works based upon the works.
- Distribute copies or phonorecords of the work to the public by sale or other transfer of ownership, or by rental, lease, or lending.
- Perform the work publicly, in the case of literary, musical, dramatic, and choreographic works, pantomimes, motion pictures, and other audiovisual works.
- Display the copyrighted work publicly, in the case of literary, musical, dramatic, and choreographic works, pantomimes, and pictorial, graphic, or sculptural works, including the individual images of a motion picture or other audiovisual work.
- In the case of sound recordings, perform the work publicly by means of a digital audio transmission.
- In addition, certain authors of works of visual art have the rights of attribution and integrity as described in Section 106A of the 1976 Copyright Act.

It is illegal for anyone to violate any of the rights provided by the copyright law to the owner of a copyright. These rights, however, are not unlimited in scope. Sections 107 through 121 of the 1976 Copyright Act establish limitations on these rights. In some cases, these limitations are specified exemptions from copyright liability. One major limitation is the doctrine of "fair use," which is given a statutory basis in section 107 of the 1976 Copyright Act. In other instances, the limitation takes the form of a "compulsory license" under which certain limited uses of copyrighted works are permitted upon payment of specified royalties and compliance with statutory conditions.

Copyright Claims

Copyright protection subsists from the time the work is created in fixed form. The copyright in the work of authorship immediately becomes the property of the author who created the work. Only the author, or those deriving their rights through the author, can rightfully claim copyright.

In the case of works made for hire, the employer and not the employee is considered to be the author. Section 101 of the 1976 copyright law defines a "work made for hire" as:

1. A work prepared by an employee within the scope of his or her employment; or
2. A work specially ordered or commissioned for use as:

• If the parties expressly agree in a written instrument signed by them that the work shall be considered a work made for hire.
• A contribution to a collective work.
• A part of a motion picture or other audiovisual work.
• A translation.
• A supplementary work.
• A compilation.
• An instructional text.
• A test.
• Answer material for a test.
• An atlas.

The authors of a joint work are co-owners of the copyright in the work, unless there is an agreement to the contrary.

A copyright in each separate contribution to a periodical or other collective work is distinct from a copyright in the collective work as a whole and vests initially with the author of the contribution.

Two General Principles

Mere ownership of a book, manuscript, painting, or any other copy or phonorecord does not give the possessor the copyright. The law provides that transfer of ownership of any material object that embodies a protected work does not of itself convey any rights in the copyright — Minors may claim copyrights, but state laws may regulate the business dealings involving copyrights owned by minors.

....

Copyright and the National Origin of the Work

Copyright protection is available for all unpublished works, regardless of the nationality or domicile of the author. Published works are eligible for copyright protection in the United States if any one of the following conditions is met:

• On the date of first publication, one or more of the authors is a national or domiciliary of the United States, or is a national, domiciliary, or sovereign authority of a treaty party, or is a stateless person wherever that person may be domiciled; or a treaty party is a country or intergovernmental organization other than the United States that is a party to an international agreement.

• The work is first published in the United States or in a foreign nation that, on the date of first publication, is a treaty party. For purposes of this condition, a work that is published in the United States or a treaty party within 30 days after publication in a foreign nation that is not a treaty party shall be considered to be first published in the United States or such treaty party, as the case may be; or the work is a sound recording that was first fixed in a treaty party; or

• The work is a pictorial, graphic, or sculptural work that is incorporated in a building or other structure, or an architectural work that is embodied in a building and the building or structure is located in the United States or a treaty party; or the work is first published by the United Nations or any of its specialized agencies, or by the Organization of American States; or

• The work is a foreign work that was in the public domain in the United States prior to 1996 and its copyright was restored under the 1994 Uruguay Round Agreements Act (URAA).

What Works are Protected?

A copyright protects "original works of authorship" that are fixed in a tangible form of expression. The fixation need not be directly perceptible so long as it may be communicated with the aid of a machine or device.

Copyrightable works include the following categories:

• Literary works.
• Musical works, including any accompanying words.
• Dramatic works, including any accompanying music.
• Pantomimes and choreographic works.
• Pictorial, graphic, and sculptural works.
• Motion pictures and other audiovisual works.
• Sound recordings.
• Architectural works.

These categories should be viewed broadly. For example, computer programs and most "compilations" may be registered as "literary works"; maps and architectural plans may be registered as "pictorial, graphic, and sculptural works."

What is Not Protected by a Copyright

Several categories of material are generally not eligible for federal copyright protection. These include, among others:

• Works that have not been fixed in a tangible form of expression (for example, choreographic works that have not been notated or recorded, or improvisational speeches or performances that have not been written or recorded).

• Titles, names, short phrases, and slogans; familiar symbols or designs; mere variations of typographic ornamentation, lettering, or coloring; mere listings of ingredients or contents.

• Ideas, procedures, methods, systems, processes, concepts, principles, discoveries, or devices, as distinguished from a description, explanation, or illustration.

• Works consisting entirely of information that is common property and containing no original authorship (for example: standard calendars, height and weight charts, tape measures and rulers, and lists or tables taken from public documents or other common sources).

How to Get a Copyright

A copyright is secured automatically upon creation. The way in which copyright protection is secured is frequently misunderstood. No publication or registration or other action in the Copyright Office is required to secure a copyright. There are, however, certain definite advantages to registration.

A copyright is secured automatically when the work is created, and a work is "created" when it is fixed in a copy or phonorecord for the first time. "Copies" are material objects from which a work can be read or visually perceived either directly or with the aid of a machine or device, such as books, manuscripts, sheet music, film, videotape, or microfilm. "Phonorecords" are material objects embodying fixations of sounds (excluding, by statutory definition, motion picture soundtracks), such as cassette tapes, CDs, or LPs. Thus, for example, a song (the "work") can be fixed in sheet music ("copies") or in phonograph disks ("phonorecords"), or both.

Publication

Publication is no longer the key to obtaining a federal copyright as it was under the Copyright Act of 1909. However, publication remains important to copyright owners.

The 1976 Copyright Act defines publication as follows:

"Publication" is the distribution of copies or phonorecords of a work to the public by sale or other transfer of ownership, or by rental, lease, or lending. The offering to distribute copies or phonorecords to a group of persons for purposes of further distribution, public performance, or public display constitutes publication. A public performance or display of a work does not of itself constitute publication.

Before 1978, a federal copyright was generally secured by the act of publication with notice of copyright, assuming compliance with all other relevant statutory conditions. U. S. works in the public domain on January 1, 1978, (for example, works published without satisfying all conditions for securing a federal copyright under the Copyright Act of 1909) remain in the public domain under the 1976 Copyright Act.

Certain foreign works originally published without notice had their copyrights restored under the URAA.

A federal copyright could also be secured before 1978 by the act of registration in the case of certain unpublished works and works eligible for ad interim copyright. The 1976 Copyright Act automatically extends to full term (Section 304 sets the term) copyright for all works, including those subject to ad interim copyright if ad interim registration has been made on or before June 30, 1978.

A further discussion of the definition of "publication" can be found in the legislative history of the 1976 Copyright Act. The legislative reports define "to the public" as distribution to persons under no explicit or implicit restrictions with respect to disclosure of the contents. The reports state that the definition makes it clear that the sale of phonorecords constitutes publication of the underlying work, for example, the musical, dramatic, or literary work embodied in a phonorecord. The reports also state that it is clear that any form of dissemination in which the material object does not change hands (for example, performances or displays on television) is not a publication, no matter how many people are exposed to the work. However, when copies or phonorecords are offered for sale or lease to a group of wholesalers, broadcasters, or motion picture theaters, publication does take place if the purpose is further distribution, public performance, or public display.

Publication is an important concept for several reasons:

• Works that are published in the United States are subject to mandatory deposit with the Library of Congress.

• Publication of a work can affect the limitations on the exclusive rights of the copyright owner that are set forth in Sections 107 through 121 of the 1976 Copyright Act.

• The year of publication may determine the duration of copyright protection for anonymous and pseudonymous works (when the author's identity is not revealed in the records of the Copyright Office) and for works made for hire.

Deposit requirements for registration of published works differ from those for registration of unpublished works. When a work is published, it may bear a notice of a copyright to identify the year of publication and the name of the copyright owner and to inform the public that the work is protected by copyright. Copies of works published before March 1, 1989, must bear the notice or risk loss of copyright protection. See discussion on "Notice of Copyright" below.

Notice of Copyright

The use of a copyright notice is no longer required under U. S. law, although it is often beneficial. Because prior law did contain such a requirement, however, the use of notice is still relevant to the copyright status of older works.

Notice was required under the 1976 Copyright Act. This requirement was eliminated when the United States adhered to the Berne Convention, effective March 1, 1989. Although works published without notice before that date could have entered the public domain in the United States, the URAA restores a copyright in certain foreign works originally published without notice. For further information about copyright amendments in the URAA, request Circular 38b.

The Copyright Office does not take a position on whether copies of works first published with notice before March 1, 1989, which are distributed on or after March 1, 1989, must bear the copyright notice.

Use of the notice may be important because it informs the public that the work is protected by copyright, identifies the copyright owner, and shows the year of first publication. Furthermore, in the event that a work is infringed, if a proper notice of copyright appears on the published copy or copies to which a defendant in a copyright infringement suit had access, then no weight shall be given to such a defendant's interposition of a defense based on innocent infringement in mitigation of actual or statutory damages, except as provided in Section 504(c)(2) of the copyright law. Innocent infringement occurs when the infringer did not realize that the work was protected.

The use of the copyright notice is the responsibility of the copyright owner and does not require advance permission from, or registration with, the Copyright Office.

Form of Notice for Visually Perceptible Copies

The notice for visually perceptible copies should contain all of the following three elements:

1. The symbol © (the letter C in a circle), or the word "Copyright," or the abbreviation "Copr."; and

2. The year of first publication of the work. In the case of compilations or derivative works incorporating previously published material, the year date of first publication of the compilation or derivative work is sufficient. The year date may be omitted where a pictorial, graphic, or sculptural work, with accompanying textual matter, if any, is reproduced in or on greeting cards, postcards, stationery, jewelry, dolls, toys, or any useful article; and

3. The name of the owner of a copyright in the work, or an abbreviation by which the name can be recognized, or a generally known alternative designation of the owner.

Example: © 2002 John Doe

The "C in a circle" notice is used only on "visually perceptible copies." Certain kinds of works — for example, musical, dramatic, and literary works — may be fixed not in "copies" but by means of sound in an audio recording. Since audio recordings such as audio tapes and phonograph disks are "phonorecords" and not "copies," the "C in a circle" notice is not used to indicate protection of the underlying musical, dramatic, or literary work that is recorded.

Form of Notice for Phonorecords of Sound Recordings

Sound recordings are defined in the law as "works that result from the fixation of a series of musical, spoken, or other sounds, but not including the sounds accompanying a motion picture or other audiovisual work." Common examples include recordings of music, drama, or lectures. A sound recording is not the same as a phonorecord. A phonorecord is the physical object in which works of authorship are embodied. The word "phonorecord" includes cassette tapes, CDs, LPs, 45 r p m disks, as well as other formats.

The notice for phonorecords embodying a sound recording should contain all of the following three elements:

1. The symbol (P) (the letter P in a circle); and

2. The year of first publication of the sound recording; and

3. The name of the owner of a copyright in the sound recording, or an abbreviation by which the name can be recognized, or a generally known alternative designation of the owner. If the producer of the sound recording is named on the phonorecord label or container and if no other name appears in conjunction with the notice, the producer's name shall be considered a part of the notice.

Example: (P) 2002 ABC Records Inc.

Since questions may arise from the use of variant forms of the notice, you may wish to seek legal advice before using any form of the notice other than those given here.

Position of Notice

The copyright notice should be affixed to copies or phonorecords in such a way as to "give reasonable notice of the claim of copyright." The three elements of the notice should ordinarily appear together on the copies or phonorecords or on the phonorecord label or container. The Copyright Office has issued regulations concerning the form and position of the copyright notice in the Code of Federal Regulations (37 CFR Section 201.20). See their Web site for more details.

Publications Incorporating U. S. Government Works

Works by the U. S. Government are not eligible for U. S. copyright protection. For works published on and after March 1, 1989, the previous notice requirement for works consisting primarily of one or more U. S. Government works has been eliminated. However, use of a notice on such a work will defeat a claim of innocent infringement as previously described provided the notice also includes a statement that identifies either those portions of the work in which a copyright is claimed or those portions that constitute U. S. Government material.

Example: © 2002 Jane Brown. Copyright claimed in Chapters 7-10, exclusive of U. S. Government maps

Copies of works published before March 1, 1989, that consist primarily of one or more works of the U.S. Government, should have a notice and the identifying statement.

Unpublished Works

The author or copyright owner may wish to place a copyright notice on any unpublished copies or phonorecords that leave his or her control.

Example: Unpublished work © 2002 Jane Doe

Omission of the Notice and Errors in Notice

The 1976 Copyright Act attempted to ameliorate the strict consequences of failure to include notice under prior law. It contained provisions that set out specific corrective steps to cure omissions or certain errors in notice. Under these provisions, an applicant had 5 years after publication to cure omission of notice or certain errors. Although these provisions are technically still in the law, their impact has been limited by the amendment making notice optional for all works published on and after March 1, 1989.

The Life of a Copyright

A work that is created (fixed in tangible form for the first time) on or after January 1, 1978, is automatically protected from the moment of its creation and is ordinarily given a term enduring for the author's life plus an additional 70 years after the author's death. In the case of "a joint work prepared by two or more authors who did not work for hire," the term lasts for 70 years after the last surviving author's death. For works made for hire, and for anonymous and pseudonymous works (unless the author's identity is revealed in Copyright Office records), the duration of copyright will be 95 years from publication or 120 years from creation, whichever is shorter.

Works Originally Created Before January 1, 1978, but Not Published or Registered by That Date.

These works have been automatically brought under the statute and are now given federal copyright protection. The duration of copyright in these works will generally be computed in the same way as for works created on or after January 1, 1978: The life-plus-70 or 95/120-year terms will apply to them as well. The law provides that in no case will the term of copyright for works in this category expire before December 31, 2002, and for works published on or before December 31, 2002, the term of copyright will not expire before December 31, 2047.

Under the law in effect before 1978, a copyright was secured either on the date a work was published with a copyright notice or on the date of registration if the work was registered in unpublished form. In either case, the copyright endured for a first term of 28 years from the date it was secured. During the last (28th) year of the first term, the copyright was eligible for renewal. The Copyright Act of 1976 extended the renewal term from 28 to 47 years for copyrights that were subsisting on January 1, 1978, or for pre-1978 copyrights restored under the URAA, making these works eligible for a total protection term of 75 years. Public Law 105-298, enacted on October 27, 1998, further extended the renewal term of copyrights still subsisting on that date by an additional 20 years, providing for a renewal term of 67 years and a total term protection of 95 years.

Public Law 102-307, enacted on June 26, 1992, amended the 1976 Copyright Act to provide for automatic renewal of the term of copyrights secured between January 1, 1964, and December 31, 1977. Although the renewal term is automatically provided, the Copyright Office does not issue a renewal certificate for these works unless a renewal application and fee are received and registered in the Copyright Office.

Public Law 102-307 makes renewal registration optional. Thus, filing for renewal registration is no longer required in order to extend the original 28-year copyright term to the full 95 years. However, some benefits accrue from making a renewal registration during the 28th year of the original term.

Transfer of a Copyright

Any or all of the copyright owner's exclusive rights or any subdivision of those rights may be transferred, but the transfer of exclusive rights is not valid unless that transfer is in writing and signed by the owner of the rights conveyed or such owner's duly authorized agent. Transfer of a right on a nonexclusive basis does not require a written agreement.

A copyright may also be conveyed by operation of law and may be bequeathed by will or pass as personal property by the applicable laws of intestate succession.

A copyright is a personal property right, and it is subject to the various state laws and regulations that govern the ownership, inheritance, or transfer of personal property as well as terms of contracts or conduct of business. For information about relevant state laws, consult an attorney.

Transfers of copyrights are normally made by contract. The U.S. Copyright Office does not have any forms for such transfers. The law does provide for the recordation in the Copyright Office of transfers of copyright ownership. Although recordation is not required to make a valid transfer between the parties, it does provide certain legal advantages and may be required to validate the transfer as against third parties.

Termination of Transfers

Under the previous law, the copyright in a work reverted to the author, if living, or if the author was not living, to other specified beneficiaries, provided a renewal claim was registered in the 28th year of the original term. The present law drops the renewal feature except for works already in the first term of statutory protection when the present law took effect. Instead, the present law permits termination of a grant of rights after 35 years under certain conditions by serving written notice on the transferee within specified time limits.

For works already under statutory copyright protection before 1978, the present law provides a similar right of termination covering the newly added years that extended the former maximum term of the copyright from 56 to 95 years.

International Copyright Protection and Registration

There is no such thing as an "international copyright" that will automatically protect an author's writings throughout the entire world. Protection against unauthorized use in a particular country depends, basically, on the national laws of that country. However, most countries do offer protection to foreign works under certain conditions, and these conditions have been greatly simplified by international copyright treaties and conventions. For further information and a list of countries that maintain copyright relations with the United States, request Circular 38a, "International Copyright Relations of the United States."

In general, copyright registration is a legal formality intended to make a public record of the basic facts of a particular copyright. However, registration is not a condition of copyright protection. Even though registration is not a requirement for protection, the copyright law provides several inducements or advantages to encourage copyright owners to make registration. Among these advantages are the following:

• Registration establishes a public record of the copyright claim. Before an infringement suit may be filed in court, registration is necessary for works of U. S. origin.

• If made before or within 5 years of publication, registration will establish *prima facie* evidence in court of the validity of the copyright and of the facts stated in the certificate.

• If registration is made within 3 months after publication of the work or prior to an infringement of the work, statutory damages and attorney's fees will be available to the copyright owner in court actions. Otherwise, only an award of actual damages and profits is available to the copyright owner.

• Registration allows the owner of the copyright to record the registration with the U. S. Customs Service for protection against the importation of infringing copies.

• Registration may be made at any time within the life of the copyright. Unlike the law before 1978, when a work has been registered in unpublished form, it is not necessary to make another registration when the work becomes published, although the copyright owner may register the published edition, if desired.

Who May File for a Copyright?

The following persons are legally entitled to submit an application form:

• The author. This is either the person who actually created the work or, if the work was made for hire, the employer or other person for whom the work was prepared.

• The copyright claimant. The copyright claimant is defined in Copyright Office regulations as either the author of the work or a person or organization that has obtained ownership of all the rights under the copyright initially belonging to the author. This category includes a person or organization that has obtained by contract the right to claim legal title to the copyright in an application for copyright registration.

• The owner of exclusive right(s). Under the law, any of the exclusive rights that make up a copyright and any subdivision of them can be transferred and owned separately, even though the transfer may be limited in time or place of effect. The term "copyright owner" with respect to any one of the exclusive rights contained in a copyright refers to the owner of that particular right. Any owner of an exclusive right may apply for registration of a claim in the work.

• The duly authorized agent of such author, other copyright claimant, or owner of exclusive right(s). Any person authorized to act on behalf of the author, other copyright claimant, or owner of exclusive rights may apply for registration.

There is no requirement that applications be prepared or filed by an attorney.

Copyright Application Forms

For Original Registration

Form PA: for published and unpublished works of the performing arts (musical and dramatic works, pantomimes and choreographic works, motion pictures, and other audiovisual works).

Form SE: for serials, works issued or intended to be issued in successive parts bearing numerical or chronological designations and intended to be continued indefinitely (periodicals, newspapers, magazines, newsletters, annuals, journals, etc.).

Form SR: for published and unpublished sound recordings.

Form TX: for published and unpublished nondramatic literary works.

Form VA: for published and unpublished works of the visual arts (pictorial, graphic, and sculptural works, including architectural works).

Form G/DN: a specialized form to register a complete month's issues of a daily newspaper when certain conditions are met.

Short Form/SE and Form SE/GROUP: specialized SE forms for use when certain requirements are met.

Short Forms TX, PA, and VA: short versions of applications for original registration.

Form GATT and Form GATT/GRP: specialized forms to register a claim in a work or group of related works in which U. S. copyright was restored under the URAA.

For Renewal Registration

Form RE: for claims to renew a copyright in works copyrighted under the law in effect through December 31, 1977 (1909 Copyright Act) and registered during the initial 28-year copyright term.

Form RE Addendum: accompanies Form RE for claims to renew copyright in works copyrighted under the 1909 Copyright Act but never registered during their initial 28-year copyright term.

For Corrections

Form CA: for supplementary registration to correct or amplify information given in the Copyright Office record of an earlier registration.

For a Group of Contributions to Periodicals

Form GR/CP: an adjunct application to be used for registration of a group of contributions to periodicals in addition to an application Form TX, PA, or VA.

How to Obtain Copyright Application Forms and Information About Fees

All Copyright Office forms are available on the Copyright Office Web site in PDF fill-in version. Go to *www.copyright.gov/forms/* and follow the instructions. The fill-in forms allow you to enter information while the form is displayed on the screen by using Adobe Acrobat Reader PDF file reader, which is available at *www.adobe.com*. You may then print the completed form and mail it to the Copyright Office. Fill-in forms provide a clean, sharp printout for your records and for filing with the Copyright Office.

Copyright Office fees are subject to change. For current fees, check the Copyright Office Web site at *www.copyright.gov*. You can also write the Copyright Office, or call (202) 707-3000.

Information by regular mail: Write to:

Library of Congress
Copyright Office
Publications Section, LM-455
101 Independence Avenue, S.E.
Washington, D.C. 20559-6000

Chapter Notes

Tips & Tricks

Whether you're a company of one or a company of 100, you want people to remember you.

In this chapter, we look at marketing and operating tips offered by Steve Yankee of *Video Success Secrets*. Steve brings to the table his in-depth knowledge about customer service, corporate identity, marketing, video demos, advertising, and much more. Also included are sample forms and contracts that you can adapt for your business.

Four Magic Phrases That Will Help Your Business Prosper

It shouldn't be a surprise to you that language plays a key role in how we provide service. Language can reflect our view of a client. It can also properly identify clients because clients are the sole reason for our existence. If you don't have clients, it stands to reason you will not be providing your services.

Words are powerful. Saying the right things can certainly build up your customers' confidence in you and their perception of your abilities. But when the wrong expressions are used, the total opposite becomes true. In this case, the old adage, "first impressions count", applies.

How do you build client confidence? First, as the old joke goes, "eschew deliberate obfuscation". In other words, keep it simple. Teach yourself to use simple, direct words. Your verbal expressions really do have the ability to make a significant difference. For instance, here's a great phrase: I'll take care of that for you. What does this statement say? It inspires customer confidence, and also improves your sense of self-worth. By forcing you to act on the customers' behalf, these words enable you to perceive yourself as an important part of your business.

Do you have employees? Teach them the same seven magical words: I'll take care of that for you. You'll get the same results: Employees that perceive their actions as critical to the business and that are focused on providing a good job for your clients. You'll find that your customer's confidence level will skyrocket, and your employees will feel like an important part of the business. Can you remember the last time you heard the words, "I'll take full responsibility?"

If you continually protect yourself from criticism by avoiding words such as these, you can be certain no one else in your company will ever utter them either! However, when you have established yourself as the person ultimately responsible for the exchange between your company and your client, you will find yourself going to great lengths to be sure no mistakes are made. Lead by example.

These are good words for you and your staff, too. "I'll take full responsibility." Learn them for yourself; teach them to your employees; and live by them.

I can't even begin to tell you how many meetings and proposals I've attended or proposals I've heard where the lead presenter finished making his or her sales pitch, delivered the unsigned contract, murmured a few final thoughts on budgets, schedules, details, and then sat down without saying this next magic phrase. I resolved that whenever I made a presentation to someone, whether it was selling them a $500,000 corporate advertising program or a half dozen copies of a videotape, I would always end it with the words, Mr. (or Ms.) Client, we want your business!

Saying, "We want your business", not only makes the message clear but that the customer counts. Far too many businesses tend to think of their clients as an annoying interference. Why should a client have to assume that you want their business when it's your place to tell them that you do?

Think about this one for a moment. How would you feel if you called a supplier and for a quote and they said, "John, we'd really like to have your business." Would you feel wanted? Would you feel special? Would you feel that regardless of how loyal you were to your usual suppliers, that you just might give these guys a shot at handling your business?

"Thank you for thinking about us" is a short, direct sentence that encapsulates what business is really all about. When a client enters your facility or calls you with a purchase in mind, they are, in effect, paying your business a compliment. And when you or your employees use these words, you will have a better understanding of the customer service relationship — and everyone will feel good about the sale.

I firmly believe that every business — whether it's a one-person tape duplication company, a two-person wedding video service, or a multi-billion dollar manufacturing corporation — has only one reason for existing, and that is to make something happen for the customer by providing good value, and finishing on time. Your clients need to be reassured that you'll do whatever needs to be done. Your words can work wonders. They can create confidence and establish better customer relationships. And those two hallmarks of good business will ensure that your customers will keep coming back for more of your good work and your good service attitude.

Put Your Best Face Forward: How to Make Your Company Look Its Best

How you present your company, particularly in a first-time situation, has a lot to do with how you're perceived in the marketplace. You may be an absolute whiz with your equipment, and you may be a virtual expert in your chosen field; but if your company looks like a bunch of amateurs, it may not get the respect that it rightfully deserves.

If you've ever worked for a big corporation, no doubt you've been specifically told how to use their logo, what typeface to use for their name, and what corporate colors you must use for reproduction. You may even have been handed a corporate graphics standards binder, replete with color swatches and exacting dimensions of everything from door signs to envelopes. The name of the game is corporate identity. And it's just as important for you as it is for any Fortune 500 company.

Whether you're a company of one or a company of 100, you want people to remember you. You want to look like you know what you're doing. You want to look stable, creative, and professional. When you strip away all the clutter and marketing gobbledygook, the real purpose of a corporate identification program is to produce a system of graphics that is professional, attractive, and that will enhance the image of the firm. Such a program should take in all aspects of visual communications, including your stationery, advertising, packaging, brochures, signage, trade show booth design, and other printed material that will be viewed by both current and potential clients — not to mention your tape and CD labels, your animated logo used on-screen, and even the equipment labels on your cameras, tripods and lights.

Okay, so you're not quite at the level of General Motors or Microsoft. It doesn't matter what size you are. Establishing and maintaining your corporate identification is very important in your marketplace, whether you're doing business on a local, regional, or national scale.

Let me tell you how we made my last company look much larger than it was. Great Lakes Video Services was incorporated about a dozen years ago. At the time of our inception, the staff consisted of my partner Randy, two part-time technicians, me. We had two small offices in a side street office building.

We were small. But we wanted to look larger than we were. We wanted to look like we were well-established (which we weren't), savvy (which we were), professional (yep), businesslike (ditto), and creative (sure!). One of the first things we did after setting up the videotape duplication rack and plugging the editing suite together was to hire a professional designer and have him develop a logo. Simple, strong, colorful and eye-catching, it featured our name and a graphic device that resembled both a wave (Great Lakes. Get it?) and an artfully draped piece of videotape. We decided on our corporate colors — strong shades of blue (for water) and green (for money), and locked in a corporate typeface, one that would not vary, regardless of where it was to be used.

We proceeded to put our new corporate identity/logo on *everything* we could think of: shipping boxes, letterhead, business cards, envelopes, order forms, mailing labels, tape box labels, cassette tops, spine labels, rate cards, service brochures, invoices. Even our equipment identification stickers carried the message in a consistent fashion. Even though Randy (the business and finance guy) winced at the cost of three-color printing for throwaway shipping labels, I persisted. If we wanted to convey the image that we were big, slick, and could deliver, we had to consistently look that way and it worked. The corporate identity we established accomplished its purpose. We were perceived as having our act together. Prospects trusted us with their work. We were treated as professionals, and our business grew quickly.

The frightening thing about public perception is that we could have been totally unhinged and thoroughly unprofessional, working in our garages or basements with antiquated equipment, but our graphic identity made us look like we knew what we were doing. Hence, people trusted us with their work. And when we did a good job, they kept coming back. And we prospered because of it.

The lesson here is to remember to present your customers and prospects with a strong, consistent image. Fragmented or sporadic adherence to this idea ultimately damages your corporate credibility. Decide what you want to be in the minds of your public. Take the time to develop a corporate identity program that says who you are and what you do, and exudes professionalism. And when you've got it, use it! Emblazon your name on everything from labels to baseball caps, ads to vehicles, business cards to building signs. Consistency is the name of the game.

How to Produce a Dynamite Video Demo

If you don't have a video demo, or you've got one that isn't doing the job, don't feel like the Lone Ranger. A good video demo is a rare commodity in our business, simply because we're like the shoemaker of legend. Many times we're simply too busy making shoes for other people to take the time to put shoes on our own [barefoot] children. If you want to run with the big dogs instead of staying on the porch, you've simply got to take the time. A good video demo, properly planned, produced, and distributed, can win you a lot of profitable new business.

What is a video demo, anyway? Contrary to what you might think, a video demo is not a random collection of snippets and scenes from video productions you've already shot and sold. Even though we've all cut and pasted and used these types of scenes before, for all intents and purposes, it is not a real video demo, primarily because "demo" stands for demonstration — not for a miscellaneous collection of unrelated scenes. The first mistake people make is trying to move too fast.

The first big mistake most producers make is to hurriedly throw a demo together because a client wants to see it immediately. The second biggest mistake is to grab unrelated or imperfect bits of video footage — bits that don't convey the message you need to relate to your prospect or suitably showcase your production quality — and hope, somehow, that it will suffice. It used to, back in the days when a video producer was the only qualification you needed to work on a video. Video is no longer a voodoo technology. Most everyone owns a VCR, if not a consumer camcorder, and has the basic knowledge of how videos are put together. With the advent of DV video and evermore powerful computer NLE editing systems, consumers have even more exposure. Far and away, though, the very biggest mistake you can make when you assemble your video demo is to center the attention on yourself, and not your client.

Your Demo Must Be Client-Centered

Let me elaborate. I've talked to hundreds of video producers. Many of them wonder why they're not bursting at the seams with profitable jobs. Most of the time it's due to a common fault. Too many video producers focus their marketing efforts on themselves, their own talents, equipment, and on what they're selling — not on the prospect and why he or she is buying the product.

Your video demo must use what I call client-centered marketing to get people to come knocking on your door after seeing it.

Client-centered marketing is very simple. All you have to understand is the difference between features and benefits. Features are about you and your product or service. Saying, "We use 3-chip broadcast quality cameras", is a feature. Benefits are the results that your products or services offer to your prospects. It would be far better to tell your client that their production is captured flawlessly, in perfect color and sharp focus (which is the benefit of using a 3-chip camera) than to tell them you use 3-chip cameras, and letting it go at that.

I want you to make a real point to remember that whether you're making a new demo tape or writing a sales letter or talking on the phone to a new prospect, you must use *benefits* to sell to their wants and desires.

And that's the first commandment of making a dynamite video demo: focus on the gained benefits of using your services, not on the features of you, your equipment or your company.

Here are a few more commandments you need to follow:

Your video demo must be planned properly. Creating an effective demo is not a one-day job. It will take some time to create and execute a video program that will really do the job you want it to do and reach the audience with which you wish to do business. It doesn't help to show wedding scenes on a demo aimed at corporations, or vice versa. Always keep the needs of your target audiences foremost in your mind. Your demo must be produced carefully and exemplify your very best work. No glitches, no bad camera moves, no bad edits. Simply the best you have, presented in a logical sequence.

Your demo tape must have a call-to-action. It must offer something to make the client respond, and respond now! It (or the note or letter that accompanies it) should contain a limited-time discount offer, a coupon good for a dozen free duplicate copies of the finished production, or some value-added benefit that makes the prospect reach for the phone to call and book you *now*.

You must get your demo tape in front of the people you want for customers. Like any marketing tool, a video demo is useless unless you get it out there working for you constantly. Who should get it? Anyone that you contact, or who contacts you, and requests more information about your company and your video capabilities. Mail it, or deliver it yourself. Get it out there where it can be seen, appreciated, and responded to.

Your video demo may be the demo to end all demos. But you've got to remember that people can be lazy or unwilling to commit to a video project. While your demo will certainly get interest, by itself, it's usually not enough to get them to call you. So you've got to realize the value of proper follow-up. That includes phone calls, postcards, and even a second or third sales letter, if required.

How to Get the Most From Your Yellow Page Advertising

The Yellow Pages are a terrific medium because of one simple reason: They are a directive medium (as opposed to a reactive medium, like a newspaper ad or TV spot). In other words, people use them when they're ready to buy! This means you can (and should) load up your ad with everything you want to say about your capabilities and services. People read *every* word because for the most part, they've already decided to buy, and your Yellow Page ad is the best possible chance to get them to call you so you can close the sale. How much should you spend in the Yellow Pages?

There's really only one rule applying to advertising budgets for the Yellow Pages that you should follow, if you can afford to do so: Have a larger ad than the rest of your competition because when you have the largest ad, 30 percent of Yellow Pages shoppers, who are motivated, ready-to-buy people, will call you first.

You should be aware that Yellow Page sales reps are notoriously close-mouthed. They won't volunteer any information about how big your competitors' ad is going to be. They will not tell you even if you ask them. However, they will normally provide you with this information if you ask them a simple [trick] question: "What size ad do I need to have the 'first position' on the page?" There is no guarantee that one of your competitors won't ask the same question, of course, but this is one way to find out what the competition is doing up to this point.

If you're just starting to advertise, and your competitor is already advertising with a display ad, you can leapfrog over his ad fairly easily and take the pole position by using a little strategy. When buying a bigger ad, most people double their present ad size. Look at the Yellow Pages, see what your competition is doing, and take out an ad two sizes bigger than the largest current ad. Suddenly, you'll be the biggest advertiser and will automatically receive more inquiries, which will lead to more sales, more work, more profits, and more fun for you.

There are two things that will help your hard-working ad work even better. The first is using a second color. It costs you more but adding it improves readership threefold. Second, rather than just having a simple ad, run a thin line around the ad, do something tricky with the as boarders (e.g., make it look like a length of videotape, or a string of chaser lights, or perforations on a roll of movie film). Or, if possible, incorporate your artwork into it; make the ad as eye-catching as possible. Ask your rep for ad design help and assistance with copy writing.

How to Develop a Successful Direct Mail Program

Direct Mail (DM) is anything you mail, hand, or present to someone to introduce your business, your services, or to ask for an order. As you can see, direct mail covers a very wide range of media and includes everything from a simple postcard to a multi-page letter, series of letters, newsletter, or any item mailed to a customer or prospect. Why use direct mail? Two good reasons: It is relatively cheap, *and* it gets results. What kind of results?

For direct response-oriented materials (those which you want to send out in order to make people buy something), here are normal response rates,

Advertising Response Rate Percentages

Display Ads vs. Direct Mail	Low	High
% responding to display advertising	0.001	1.0
Closing rates for replies to these ads	0.5	1.5
% responding to single direct mailing	0.25	5.0
Closing rate for replies to single DM	1.5	2.5

contrasted with normal display advertising rates:

As you can see, the response and closing rates for direct mail are higher than those for classified or display advertising, simply because direct mail is usually more targeted than print advertising, which is why I like direct mail better than I like advertising. It gets better results.

But do you see how things work here? It's what we call the law of large numbers. The same principles that rule live sales calls also work with direct mail. (Make a hundred cold telephone calls; out of those calls, 10 people will agree to read more information or make an appointment with you; out of that 10, one will give you a project). On a typical promotion, you may send out 1,000 postcards with a specific offer. You may get as few as a quarter of one percent (2.5 people) to respond, or you may get as many as five percent (50 people) to respond. And of those 2.5 or 50 people, you may close one order or less, or 12.5 orders or more. It's definitely a numbers game and not an exact science.

Direct mail can be something as basic as a one-page letter, or get as fancy as a whole bunch of items stuffed into a good-looking package. But for the most part, effective and economical direct mail campaign you can use to get started will consist of a series of letters (or flyers or postcards) sent to targeted prospects.

Here's how it works: Let's assume that you've decided to do a mailing to insurance agents in your area, seeking new clients for your home inventory video services. You can look in the Yellow Pages to put your mailing list together, but these listings won't tell you the name of the person you want to contact. Depending on the size of the firm, this may be the president, the V.P. of sales, or the office manager. So you may have to do some phone work to find out who should get your direct mail offer; just call them up, explain *briefly* what you're doing, and ask for the name and title of the person who should receive this information.

An alternative is to get a copy of your local Chamber of Commerce's membership list or business directory, which are available in most cities.

Okay, so you've got some names? Now what? Well, one simple (yet very effective) direct mail package typically has four elements: First is a personalized letter. Second is your business card. Third is a flyer which, for example, would present the many benefits of retaining you as a video resource. Lastly, the package would contain a prepaid business reply postcard.

Now, assuming you've sent your articles to the right person in the organization, you have three obstacles to overcome:

First, you've got to get that letter opened. Second, you've got to get that letter read by the right person. And third, you've got to get that person to take some action!

How do you entice a prospect to open a direct mail piece? You can spend hours and hours writing and editing and laboring over a great sales letter, but your time will be wasted if your prospect doesn't open it. Remember, businesses get dozens of direct mail offers every week, most of which is unsolicited. Therefore, your direct mail piece material is competing for your prospect's attention!

Avoid gimmicks. For business types, what traditionally works best are personalized business letters, mailed in #10 size envelopes. Don't use labels. Type the addresses right on the envelopes, or print them on with your desktop printer. You can occasionally hire someone with good penmanship to address direct mail envelopes, supplying them with blank envelopes, the proper sort of pen, and addresses. They typically receive a dime for each envelope they address.

Mail first class and use a stamp. Don't use a postage meter. Stamped mail is likely to get opened faster than metered mail. If you want to attract a lot of attention, use three or four stamps instead of one first-class stamp. Use good quality #10 envelopes with your company's name and address (logo too, if you've got one) in the upper left hand corner. If you're going after four or five prime prospects, you might try sending your materials to them by Priority Mail or FedEx, and put it in the appropriate envelope or package. It is definitely expensive, but have you ever seen anyone toss away an unopened Priority Mail pouch or Federal Express Letterpack?

And don't forget follow-up. You'll get replies: Cards will be returned, and you'll no doubt get phone calls and email, too. Follow-up on your leads *promptly* by sending the information you promised or by calling your prospects. I've seen good direct mail campaigns that have cost well into five figures sink quickly at this point because their users weren't prepared to deal with incoming leads promptly and efficiently.

How to Overcome Customer Price Objections

I got an interesting phone call the other day from a producer friend of mine, asking me how my company overcomes customer price objections. I know this is not an isolated instance because we've all run up against this at one time or another. Rather than back down immediately and run the risk of blowing your profit margin, I suggest you try this tried and proven way of finding out why a customer believes your price may be too high: Ask them!

You should use whatever tactics you feel comfortable with in order to discover the reason behind the objection, because once the customer has provided you with this information, you will be able to address the issue both intelligently and professionally.

Two factors affect a potential customer's purchasing behavior:

• Ability to buy.
• Willingness to buy.

If they can't afford and/or don't want to buy, there will be no sale.

There are several reasons that may make the customer feel your price is too high when, in actuality, it really isn't. Perhaps they only have, say, $5,000 dollars in their budget but want to purchase a service from you that normally costs $7,500. This type of price objection is fairly easy to handle. Your price isn't too high. The customer just doesn't have the money required for the sale. At this point, it's up to you, or your salesperson, to find a way to make the sale possible for the customer. You might want to suggest financing the item, for instance. Or set up a payment schedule, say three payments of $2,500 each. Or you may want to point out a similar (but less expensive) production that the customer is able to afford. Perhaps you'll have to explain that his or her budget is set unrealistically low. If so, do it gently, but do it!

What if another customer complains that your competition charges $1,000 less for a similar product or service? This type of customer conflict often occurs when you or your salesperson has named the price on an item without presenting a full picture of the very special features and benefits that it offers. By not giving them all the information on your product or service, you're giving the customer a legitimate reason to dismiss it and use an unfair comparison with your competitor.

Why is this comparison unfair? You've not given yourself the chance to point out the differences between products. You have not explained, for instance, that while your item may be priced slightly higher, it will better meet the specific needs of the customer. You need to be well-prepared for this type of confrontation. Remember to stress that, in the long run, your service or product will cost the customer less because of added values, such as special packaging, a technically better product, more capable personnel, extra coverage, free copies, or free shipping. You must always justify why your price is different than those of the competition. When addressing this difference, you should concentrate solely on the conflicting amount and not on the total price of the item or service.

You should always move on quickly with your product or service presentation, as a pause in the conversation leaves the issue open to the customer, which will allow them time to object. And once you've neared the end of the presentation, you should come straight to the point --which is to ask for the order. Remember how it starts: "Mr. Prospective Client, we really want your business." And remember — after they've signed the contract or given you that first check — don't play the big shot. Don't pretend you're doing them a favor. *Thank them for their business*. After all, your clients are the very reason you are in business.

How to Create Your Own Press Releases

Welcome to the press release: a terrific promotional tool that will cost you only a few sheets of paper, a couple of stamped envelopes, and an hour or two of your time. Don't be too quick to sneer at such a lowly marketing device; let me assure you that if you follow the simple advice I'm about to give you, you can turn a modest investment into literally hundreds of dollars worth of valuable magazine and newspaper space, which can lead directly to thousands of dollars in new business. Here's how it works:

I spent a couple of years editing newspapers and city magazines. From first-hand experience, I know full well that magazine and newspaper editors really appreciate receiving submissions and news releases from their readers. Why? It's not that local editors and writers are intrinsically lazy, it's just that they're generally snowed under in sentences, piled high with paragraphs, sinking in a sea of special features, and drowning under inescapable deadlines. It follows, then, that the more things you write and provide them for their publication, the less they have to write.

If you follow these steps, you'll be on your way to creating enhanced visibility for your company, which will lead to more and better sales opportunities, for a very modest out-of-pocket cost.

1. Prepare a mailing list. I recommend that you send news releases and photos to every local and regional newspaper and magazine in your business area. Thus, you'll need the names and addresses of publications in your area. Easy. Make a list of media names, and all address and phone numbers listed. The more the merrier! (After all, it's only going to cost you a couple pieces of paper, an envelope, and a stamp to reach each name on your list.) Then, call each of these organizations on your list, and get the name (correct spelling) of the managing editor or news editor or business news editor, who are the people you want to reach.

2. Prepare a list of newsworthy topics. Everything you do is news. Here are some suggestions for releases:

• Joined a professional organization.
• Attended a regional or national convention or trade show.
• Extended your office hours.
• Open on Saturdays.
• You are producing a new project for a prestigious local client.
• Hired a new staff person, or just promoted a staff person.
• Expanded your capabilities.
• Opened a new office or studio.

3. Get some still photos taken. You should automatically send a photograph of yourself the first time you send a release to local and regional publications. Even if they don't use it, it'll go in their picture "morgue" and be on file for later use. If you're sending in a release about a new staff person or a promotion, you should also send along a picture of that person or persons. In many other instances, print media editors will respond to your release by calling you and asking for a photo. If at all possible, you should have these ready beforehand.

4. Write and produce your press release. You don't have to be a great writer to put a news release together. There's a simple format that editors like, and you should follow it. First, use your company letterhead. If you don't have one, type your company name, complete address, and phone number(s) in the upper right-hand corner. Next, provide a release date. Type "For Immediate Release" near the top of the page. This lets editors know that they can use this information immediately. If you don't want the news released until a later date, then write what we call a "news embargo" date in its place, such as "For Release 4/1/2009."

Next, write the title or headline of the release, such as "Acme Video Now Offers Home Movie Transfers to DVD." This should be written in all capital letters (easier for editors to make it into a headline that way by counting letters, and easier for them to quickly determine the contents and/or newsworthiness).

Next, of course, write the release itself. Keep it as short as possible; typed double-spaced, it should never run longer than two pages. If your first draft runs longer, start editing. You need to cover the basics: who, what, why, where, when, and how. Always try to load the release up with feature-benefit points, though, because some magazines will print virtually every word that you send them; and you must be ready to take advantage of those opportunities.

Most newspapers and magazines will reduce all these wonderful words down to a paragraph or two at best, or a line or two at the worst. But remember, it's *free* advertising. And if you're living in a one-newspaper town, this is probably going to be big local news; you might get the whole release printed just as you wrote it, along with any pictures.

How to Organize Your Work

Organization definitely helps life run smoother; particularly if you're a typical entrepreneur with a hundred projects running all at once. There are hundreds of computer programs that are on the market today. There are pocket day-planners and even hand-held computer devices, offering All offer the same benefits. Their goal is to keep you organized. There is a simpler approach to organization and planning: Enter *The Work Wall*: Life-At-A-Glance.

Most of my script and article work is done at a large table, facing a wall in my office. Mounted on the wall is a large (4' x 5') bulletin board. I refer to this space as *my life-at-a-glance*. Stretched across the top is a row of file cards titled as follows:

• Projects in Development.
• Projects in Scripting.
• Projects in Production.
• Projects in Marketing.

Underneath are separate 4" x 6" file cards on each project with which I'm currently working. For example, the latest issue of the Video Success Newsletter, my quarterly resource guide; a mailer for an upcoming Marketing Secrets Seminar; another card on an article I'm drafting for a national magazine; cards on two ideas for new books; a half-dozen cards on current writing assignments for various clients; and a couple more cards for various marketing tools, new product packaging, or a new audio CD that I want to finish soon.

Each of these cards contains the name of the project, its job number, and the target date for completion. They are pinned under the appropriate category card. The new Corporate Identity video I'm writing for a client for example, is pinned under Projects in Scripting. When it's finished and ready for release, I'll move the card to the Projects in Production category.

I can also write down specific information on job cards. If it's a script for a client, I can jot down the date it's due, the date revisions must be finished, etc. In the case of a brochure I'm preparing for another client, I can write down the printer's name, the date it's due to the printer and the date it's due to be delivered to the client. With this system, at a glance, I can look up at the board and see the couple dozen projects that are in the shop at any given moment, and so can anyone else who needs to know. That's a big chunk of the Work Wall...but there's more.

Like you, I need a daily dose of motivation. I need to know why I'm working and what I'm working towards. My main goal is on a separate card at eye level. It reads: "To become the best source of video business training materials in North America." I see this every morning. Two years ago, my goal was to have two houses: a quiet one near the Lake Michigan coast, and another in an exciting city. My places in Grand Haven, Michigan, and Montreal more than qualify, and once the goal was met, it was time for the new one. (Remember: you can always make a new goal when you've attained your present one.) The goal is there because, just like you, I need to be constantly reminded about why I'm doing what I do. As an additional source of motivation, I've pinned up pictures of my children, my grandchild, and my girlfriend. I want to be able to help these loved ones financially and emotionally; because I see their pictures several times a day, they are a constant and silent source of motivation and inspiration.

You might be surprised to learn that your picture might well be on my work wall, too; several photos of my friends, a few fans, role models, and even pictures of my best clients adorn one corner of the wall, as does a list of all my clients' names. Each time I glance at the wall, these names and pictures serve to remind me that I'm working for them and must keep their best interests at heart.

One eye-level card reads: "The Task At Hand." This is where the list of this week's activities goes. And a card next to it lists the month's goals (sales volumes, that sort of thing) and weekly activities, like when edits are due to be completed, meetings are scheduled with clients, or interview dates/times are scheduled.

One thing the Work Wall lacks is a calendar. You should only have *one* calendar. But, then, how many calendars do you really need? Only one, and you carry it with you at all times. I use a Day Runner "Time Management System" planning book with separate time sheets for every day of the week and a separate section with two pages for every month of the year. Every meeting, every edit session, every follow-up phone call, every birthday or anniversary that I have to know about is in that calendar. You don't need a calendar at your desk, another one in your briefcase, another one on the kitchen wall, another in your study. You need one calendar that has everything combined, and you need it with you most every place you go!

My own personal, portable "life-at-a-glance" sits just to the left of my keyboard, open to today's date. Glancing down and to the left, I know exactly who I have to call and what I have to do today. Glancing up at the pictures on the wall, I know why and for whom I'm working for today.

If you're an entrepreneur, there's no doubt that you have a dozen projects that are all in various stages of completion. You might be working on a client project or ten client projects; you're attempting to prepare a news release; you're writing up a proposal for a big prospect; you've got a big job booked for the end of the month; and you've got a dinner meeting to attend this weekend.

A Work Wall is an eminently simple, cheap, and effective way to organize your work *and* your life in one fell swoop. Get yourself down to the local office discount store tomorrow morning and pick up a large bulletin board, a box of art tacks and a pack of 4" x 6" index cards. It doesn't have to be fancy. In fact, you can even cover a piece of thick foam core in an inexpensive fabric to match your office decor. All it has to do is facilitate your own individual work flow.

You may feel that you don't need a Work Wall or a carry-around calendar system. However, as a motivated businessperson looking to succeed, you will be well on your way to prosperity and success if you do. Implement techniques presented here and grow through success!

Event Planning Sheet

Please return this form no later that 2 weeks before your event.

Event contact:_____

Telephone:_____

Start time of event:_____ End time of event:_____

Location:_____

Event directions:

_____

_____

_____

_____

Special provisions and additional services requested:

_____

_____

_____

_____

_____

Sample Contract

Client:_____

Date: _____

Address:_____

Wedding Date: _____ Time: _____

We hereby submit specifications for:

A complete video production of your wedding and reception for the sum of $_____, plus any state sales tax due. It is agreed that:

1. The final edited digital master will run approximately 90 minutes to 2 hours in length. Videographer is granted full production and editorial control by the client regarding all aspects of the production. In the event

a particular segment is either not recorded, partially recorded, or not a part of the edited master tape, it is at the sole discretion of videographer as the exclusive producer of the video production.

2. Videographer will attend the wedding rehearsal and/or meet with celebrant prior to the wedding date for the purpose of arranging camera placement.

3. Videographer will remain at the reception until the expiration of the time contracted in the wedding package purchased. Videographer will notify either the bride or the groom prior to videographer's scheduled departure from the reception. The couple may, if they wish, arrange additional reception coverage at this time at the rate of $____ per additional hour. A dinner place setting will be provided for videographer at the reception. Videographer will be allowed a reasonable time for dinner. Videotaping during the dinner period will generally be confined to toasts to the bride and groom. Guests and/or wedding party members will generally not be videotaped while they are dining.

4. Production deposit is non-refundable. It is agreed that payment will be made in 3 installments as follows:

$_____ (50% production deposit; required to secure date)
$_____ (25% on wedding day or at the rehearsal)
$_____ (25% on delivery)

5. Videographer shall be the sole professional videographer at the event. Client releases and authorizes videographer to use images, names, sounds, and any reproductions and/or recordings for promotional purposes. In return, videographer agrees to use the same in good faith and in good taste.

6. The finished video will be available approximately 3 months following the wedding. Client agrees to claim finished video production within a period not to exceed 60 days from project completion. Failure to do so may incur a late penalty of 5% of the total production fee, to be added to any balance due. Client agrees that videographer holds exclusive copyrights to the production.

7. Videographer will return all deposits in the event videographer is unable to videotape the wedding or any portion of the wedding due to sudden and serious crew illness, accidents, uncontrollable and unforeseeable equipment failure, or acts of God. In such cases, videographer's lia-

bility will be limited to a maximum full refund of all client monies received.

This contract may be withdrawn by us if not accepted within 10 days.

Acceptance of contract: The above prices, specifications, and conditions are satisfactory and are hereby accepted. Videographer is authorized to do the work as specified and payment will be made as outlined above.

Client Signature _____

Client Name: _____ (Please print)

Videographer Signature: _____

Videographer Name: _____ (Please print)

Customer Follow-up Survey Form

Please check your response:

1. How would you rate our pre-event planning services?

   Good ____ Average____ Poor____

2. Did we set-up in a timely manner?

   Good ____ Average____ Poor____

3. Did we meet your expectations during your event?

   Good ____ Average____ Poor____

4. What can we do to improve our services?

   _____
   _____
   _____
   _____
   _____

5. May we use your name and contact information as a reference?

Yes ____ No____

If yes, please provide your contact information:

Name: _____

Address: _____

_____

Zip:_____

Telephone:_____

Email:_____

Signed:_____

Printed Name:_____

Chapter Notes

Financing Your Business

This chapter offers you a quick overview of some of the sources of where you can find financing for your business. From partners, family, friends, government loan programs, to credit cards, this chapter offers strategies to help you get the start-up capital you will need.

Money Sources

Where are you going to get the money to start your video service? Will you:

• Provide the money yourself from savings or existing equity?
• Take a loan from a bank or the government?
• Get a loan from friends and family?
• Provide an equity stake in your business to business partners?
• Credit cards?

There are many ways to approach the financing of your venture. I will discuss a few of them here. Keep in mind that you can use a combination of these when exploring the financing of your business.

You Have The Money

By far, the easiest way to obtain money to start your business is to provide it yourself. You might have savings that you can dip into, or you may have property with equity that you can use to borrow against. You may want to consider providing some of your savings and the rest in a loan. For example, you could provide half your start-up capital from your savings and the other half from a property equity line.

Property equity lines are relatively easy to get these days. Basically, these are secured loans that are based on the value of your property. For example, if you paid $100,000 for your house and the appraised value is $125,000, you could borrow $25,000, which is the equity that you have built in the property over time. The bank protects itself by securing the loan. This means that if you do not pay back the loan, the bank can foreclose on your property and force the sale of the property to pay back the loan.

The Bank Has The Money

The reality is that most banks will not loan you money unless you have collateral that they can use to secure a loan. You can't blame them. They are in business too, and must protect their interests. You can dress up in your Sunday suit and take your spit-polished business plan into a meeting and try to convince a banker to loan you all the money to start your venture. However, be ready for rejection.

Banks generally do not make loans for DJ services because there is no collateral stake that they can make. For example if loans are not repaid, they know that the value of used equipment, goes down fast. So, if they had loaned you money based on the new market price, they would be in the hole if they had to sell the assets to pay for delinquent loans.

The Government Has The Money

The United States Small Business Administration (SBA) might invest in your idea by providing you with a loan. However, they generally provide business planning assistance through associations like their Small Business Development Centers and The Service Corps of Retired Executives (SCORE). The government has grant money available; however, qualification parameters are constantly changing. To get an idea of what is available go to the Small Business Administrations Internet Web site at *www.sba.gov.*

*Download the Ebook, **The Government Loan Resource Guide**, at the Web site.*

Family and Friends Have The Money

Family and friends can be a good source for funds. As long as you treat these sources with respect and show them your plans, you may find an early supporter in your quest for start-up capital. Keep all business relationships professional, even if family and friends are involved.

Personal relationships can be destroyed if there is no attention paid to the business side of the relationship. If someone loans you money, sign a note of promise to pay, with the specific terms of repayment set fourth in the note. This will make for a better relationship overall because you will be showing your friend and/or family member that you are a responsible business person.

Partners

Many people form partnerships to assist in the financing of a business and to help share and limit risk. Working partners generally have a say in how the business is run; silent partners do not. There are many ways to set up partnerships. For example, in order to maintain decision control of your company, you can elect to have silent partners, whereby they will be provided an equal share of the ownership of the business in exchange for their investment.

Credit Cards

In today's credit-happy society, banks are eager to provide credit cards to almost anybody. Once you establish good credit through the credit bureaus, the banks will be sending you unsolicited applications with lines of credit and generous repayment interest rate terms. Credit cards are basically unsecured lines of credit, meaning that there is no collateral needed to obtain them. Interest rates can be higher than more conventional loans; however, they can help with some of your start-up expenses when establishing your business. As with any loan, be sure to include these loan expenses as part of your start-up expense.

Your Plan of Attack

Keep in mind that financing your business is going to be one of the most difficult aspects of starting up. It is going to demand that you establish your credibility and integrity with people. Creativity can be your key to success in regard to how you choose to approach loans from banks, government, friends, and partners.

Your business plan is your critical success tool. Your plan will tell prospective investors what your concept is and what you are all about. Don't be shy. Show your plan with pride. When asked a specific question, say, "...let's see what page that is on...", and turn to the specific page in your business plan. Once you do this, the demeanor of your prospect will change immediately.

Establish your credibility by sharing with your prospect your professional background and why you are convinced your business concept will work. Be enthusiastic and knowledgeable about your goals.

Constructive Criticism

Listen and adapt. Bankers, friends, and family might offer suggestions about how you can improve your pitch for a loan. If they do, don't get defensive. Instead adapt your business plan and loan pitch to deal with their objections. The main element in your proposal is personal selling. You are selling yourself and your ideas. In order to successfully close the sale, you will need to deal with all of the prospects objections.

Obtaining funds for your DJ service can be a daunting task. It can be a time-consuming and sometimes frustrating project. However, with persistence and organization you will prevail.

Remember, never quit!

Chapter Notes

The Web Site

www.bizventures.com/video

This chapter explains some of the products and services that you will find at the Web site, which accompanies this book. Many of the software programs are available as demos and some are free. Be sure to return your registration card so that you will be able to access the site.

Software

Project Management Software

Project management software designed to keep your project on track. What is a project?

A project is starting a video service business. Simply load a sample project into the program and then edit. I highly recommend that you use this program from the very start of your endeavors because it will help budgeting and keep you on track. The manual for this program is in a file called justdoit.pdf, for Adobe Acrobat Reader. Once installed, study the example project files to see how simple it is to create your own project(s).

. . . .

Employee Shift Scheduling Software

If you are running a multi-shift employee operation, then Scheduling Employees for Windows is a must! This award winning software program is a cinch to learn and will pay big dividends. This program is fantastic!

Safety Advisor Software

OSHA Software Application Programs

Government regulations play a key role in your activities as a video service operator. We have assembled some expert systems that you can be use to establish sections of your operations manual. Simply install the software and answers the questions. Policies will be generated for you automatically.

Safety Pays

Safety Pays is a tool developed by the Occupational Safety and Health Administration (OSHA) to assist employers in assessing the impact of occupational injuries and illnesses on their profitability. It uses a company's profit margin, the average costs of an injury or illness, and an indirect cost multiplier to project the amount of sales a company would need to generate in order to cover those costs.

Fire Safety

The Fire Safety Advisor program provides interactive expert help. It addresses OSHA's general industry standards for fire safety and emergency evacuation, and for fire fighting, fire suppression, and fire detection systems and equipment. Once installed on your PC, it asks you about office and business policies and practices. It asks follow-up questions based on your answers to prepare the guidance and write the customized plans you need.

Hazard Awareness

The Hazard Awareness Program is powerful, interactive, expert software to identify hazards in general industry workplaces. It will ask you about your workplace, and ask follow-up questions based on your answers. It will write you a customized report about possible hazards and related OSHA rules.

Safety and Health

This Expert Advisor will help you review and evaluate key aspects of your safety and health program, if you have one. If you do not have one, it could help you think about elements of a good program. It is straight-forward and very easy to use.

Occupational Safety and Health Administration (OSHA)

Here you will find various documents that will help you with OSHA inspections and assist with job-hazard analysis procedures that will become part of your operations manual.

• OSHA inspections.
• OSHA handbook for small business.
• Job hazard analysis.
• What to expect during OSHA's visit.

Posters

Here you will find government informational posters that you will be required to post in your establishment.

• Job safety poster.
• Equal opportunity poster.
• Equal opportunity poster in Spanish.
• Employee polygraph protection act poster.
• Employee family medical leave act poster.
• Employee family medical leave act poster in Spanish.

Bonus
Download the Microsoft Word and Excel spreadsheets that go with the business plan in Chapter 5, The Business Plan. Edit them and you will have your business plan ready to go!

Ebooks

We have put together a series of electronic books that you can download. This is only a partial listing, so be sure to check the site for the latest additions.

• How to Get a Trademark.
• How to Get a Patent.
• The Government Loan Resource Guide.

CD-ROM

We have a CD-ROM available for purchase with the contents of the Web site. This way you can have all the contents at your fingertips for quick access. See the registration form at the back of the book for details about how to order.

The optional CD-ROM, contains the same information and software that you will find at the Web site. We have made it available for purchase for those of you who want to have the information available first hand.

Appendix

Knowledge

This is the appendix. Here you will find supplemental information, contact lists and bibliography.

Resources

Government Resources

U.S. Small Business Administration
www.sba.gov
www.business.gov

U.S. Internal Revenue Service
www.irs.gov

U.S. Federal Trade Commission
www.ftc.gov

U.S. Department of Labor
www.dol.gov

Video Education

The following Web sites have video primers and articles. Here you will find great educational tools. *Video Success Secrets* is the site of contributing author, Steve Yankee. Get simple-to-learn training materials to improve you business.

Video Success Secrets
www.videosuccess.com

Adobe Software
www.adobe.com

Elite Video
www.elitevideo.com

How Stuff Works
www.howstuffworks.com

Pete's Video
www.petesvideo.com

Video University
www.videouniversity.com

Trade Magazines

AV Video Multimedia Producer Magazine
www.avvmmp.com

Digital Video Magazine
www.dv.com

eMedia Magazine
www.emedialive.com

PC Graphic & Video Magazine
www.pcgv.com

Videomaker Magazine
www.videomaker.com

Trade Associations

Law Enforcement Video Association
www.leva.org

Media Alliance
www.media-alliance.org

National Association of TV Arts & Sciences
www.emmyonline.org

National Association of Broadcasting
www.nabetcwa.org

National Legal Video Association
www.nlva.com

National Writers Union
www.nwu.org

Society of Motion Picture & TV Engineers
www.smpte.org

Videographer.com - Promotion service.
ww.videographer.com

Wedding and Event Videographers Association International
www.weva.com

Writers Guild of America
www.wgaeast.org

Bibliography

Business Buyer's Handbook, by Jim Calkins. Published by Oak Tree Publishing, Claremont, California.

Fundamentals of Production/Operations Management, by Harold E. Fearon. Published by West Publishing Company, Los Angeles, California.

Principles of Accounting, by Melvin Morgenstein. Published by HBJ Media Systems Corporation, New York, New York.

Marketing, by Carl McDaniel, Jr. Published by Harper & Row, New York, New York.

Marketing Management: Strategy and Cases, by Douglas J. Dalrymple. Published by John Wiley & Sons, New York, New York.

Music, Speech, High Fidelity, by William J. Strong and George R. Plitnik, Second edition. Published by Soundprint.

Music, Money and Success, by Jeffrey and Todd Brabec, Second edition. Published by Schirmer Trade Books, New York, New York.

Modern Recording Techniques, by Robert E. Runstein. Published by Howard W. Sams & Company, New York, New York.

Home Recording for Musicians, by Craig Anderton. Published by Guitar Player Books.

The Recording Studio Handbook, by John M. Woram. Published by Sagamore Publishing Company, Plainview, New York.

Audio Cyclopedia, by Howard M. Tremaine. Published by Howard W. Sams & Company, New York, New York.

Multi-Track Recording, by Brent Hurtig. Published by, GPI Publications, Cupertino, California.

Music Publishing: A Writer's Guide, by Randy Poe, Published by Writer's Digest Books, Cincinnati, Ohio.

Digital Guerrilla Video, by Avi Hoffer. Published by Miller Freeman Books, San Francisco, California.

Notes

Notes

Notes

Notes

Notes

Notes

Never Quit.

Product Registration Form

Yes! I want my free Web site access...

Date_____

Name_____

Company_____

Address_____

City_____State_____ Zip_____

Country_____

Telephone_____

Web site_____

Email (Please print clearly)_____
(Important: We will email you your Web site access code)

Where did you purchase your book?

_____

Age_____ Male_____ Female____

CD-ROM Order

Please send me *The Multimedia Cookbook: Business Start-up Guide CD-ROM* for only $24.95 plus $5.00 shipping and handling to the address above.

___ I have enclosed a check.

___ I wish to pay via credit card:

___ American Express ___ Master Card ___Visa

Card Holders Name_____

Credit Card Number_____

Expiration Date_____

Card Holders Signature_____

Mail This Completed Form To:

Venture Marketing, Inc.
Box 151
Chino Hills CA 91709

- Cut along the dotted line and mail this form -